this PLACE

A Few Notes from Home

BOOK THREE OF
THE *PLACE* TRILOGY

Around 20 years ago, I began receiving *Notes From Toad Hall* in the mail. Since then, I've saved every issue, devoting an entire shelf in my office to their preservation. With *This Place,* I'm thrilled to have an essay collection that ranges through the three plus decades that *Notes* has been gracing the mailboxes of grateful readers. There's so much I had missed and now all this gold is in one book! As one essay turns to another, we're invited to see that it's in the daily, ordinary, hard, lovely, and real places of our lives that God is with us and for us, even at the kitchen sink.

—ANDI ASHWORTH, author, *Real Love for Real Life: The Art & Work of Caring*

Reading Margie Haack is at one and the same time deeply satisfying, because we are sure she knows us, and horribly troubling, because she knows us. Like her, we are people trying hard to keep going, aware—as she writes in *This Place*—that "the rhythm of ordinary life is rarely that exciting or sensational for all who wander the wastelands of earth." Whether we enter into her world in the quiet of our own hearts, or in the company of family and friends, her words are a gift of grace, allowing us to remember what matters most—and to imagine that it is possible to still love what is ours to love, wounded people in a wounded world that we are.

—STEVEN GARBER, author of *Visions of Vocation: Common Grace for the Common Good*

In this wonderfully honest, raw, and joyful book, Margie Haack's words convey a whisper of sanity and authenticity in the midst of an otherwise clamorous world. May we all learn and grow from the window she has provided us into the life of faith.

—DAVID RICHTER, Senior Pastor, City Church East Nashville, Tennessee

I've been addicted to Margie's newsletter, *Notes from Toad Hall,* since 1997. I think it began with something about carpenter ants which made me understand this was no namby-pamby Christian writer. Here was someone who connected the broadness and the depth and the fabulous wackiness of God with that same stuff in life. She's refreshingly nuts, and is in the dirt with us, but she writes better than anyone does about that dirt. Margie has helped me grapple with the light and the dark, the confusion and the dancing that makes up figuring out how to live as a Christian. I know she talks about being influenced by Ann Lamott, but when I started reading Ann Lamott, I thought she sounded so much like Margie. *This Place* puts some of my favorite pieces together to enjoy again.

—LESLIE VAN ORSDEL, Global Head, Client Risk Engagement and Risk Assurance, Bloomberg LP

God is so great, nothing is outside of His control; He is so intimate, no detail of our lives escapes His involvement. Margie's latest book is an invitation into the ordinariness of life where we learn over and over again Christ is in all things—even a sink full of dirty dishes. If God seems absent from the commonplace of your life, Margie will help open your eyes to see Him more. In *This Place* Margie invites us into the commonness of life. But there is no boredom here. Instead, we are repeatedly confronted with the hidden glory of Christ in the most surprising of places. The One who made all things and is in all things, is also present in the dailyness of our lives. Margie has been given the eyes to reveal Him to us.

—ED HAGUE, founder, Macpro Services

Margie Haack has long been one of my favorite writers. Her occasional essays (which are sometimes as intimate as confessions, as brazen as a stand-up comedian, as glorious about the spirituality of the ordinary as a modern mystic) have come into our home for years in her wonderful *Notes from Toad Hall.* That the best of these candid, entertaining, excellently-crafted pieces are now collected and offered in this lovely volume is truly a great thing. These will inspire you to see God's hand in the ups and downs of life, help you learn to apply scripture to the mundane moments of a hectic life, and to—believe it or not—find God even in the kitchen sink.

—BYRON BORGER, co-owner, Hearts and Minds Bookstore

In this humorous and vulnerable collection of stories, Margie opens the shades of her home and invites us to see that in all stages and seasons of life, God is eager to fill even our most mundane moments with meaning and grace. As a fellow wife, mother, and chronic fixer of the world's problems, I saw glimpses of myself in her efforts to be a faithful follower of Jesus in the smallest of things: feeding her family, welcoming strangers, or losing her car in a parking lot while attempting to save the world. In her stories, we see that God is in the floorboards and in our failures, in the stairways and in our successes, and is truly Lord over even the dirtiest dishes in our souls. This is a deeply encouraging book.

—ELIZABETH BERGET, photographer, blogger, wife, mother

As exquisite as a summer evening on the back porch of Toad Hall, these are the insights that only a friend who has loved and laughed over the life she has been given can share with you. Hers is an authentic voice that makes you believe it can make a difference to think about Jesus, and a grand celebration of a tested faith that has held together through life's most absurd and familiar moments. Reading *This Place* might turn your household chores into part of the sacred dance.

—JAMES DISNEY, pastor, Bethlehem Lutheran Church, Minnetonka, MN

this PLACE

A Few Notes from Home

BOOK THREE OF
THE *PLACE* TRILOGY

A Memoir *(of sorts) by*
Margie Haack

FOREWORD BY Zack Eswine

SQUARE HALO BOOKS

In Christian art, the square halo identified a living person presumed to be a saint. Square Halo Books is devoted to publishing works that present contextually sensitive biblical studies, and practical instruction consistent with the Doctrines of the Reformation. The goal of Square Halo Books is to provide materials useful for encouraging and equipping the saints.

Cover painting by Abigail Clark

P.O. Box 18954
Baltimore, MD 21206
www.SquareHaloBooks.com

ISBN 978-1-941106-20-4
Library of Congress Control Number: 2021949020

Printed in the United States of America

for Edith

Dedicated to the memory of
Edith Schaeffer (1914–2013),
whose life and rambling
Family Letters inspired my own.

contents

FOREWORD

This book is like a sage guide, a time-tested, child-cracked nightlight vibrantly glowing in the dark hall. Margie's durable words illumine a soft-lit path through the night-watch house of our lives.

Perhaps the floors creak beneath each pajama step. We are guests, uncertain which door to open, anxious not to disturb the host, break a lamp, stub a toe. But the wise have long learned that a floor will creak no matter who steps on it, and either way, a creaking floor can handle the weight you carry. Sometimes it's the creaking things that surprise us with sturdy places to walk or to skip with wonder if you dare.

I did not venture into nightlight or walk the floors of Toad Hall. Only the "House Between" has carried my weight. Jessica and I came with our questions. Needing rest. Anxious to discern which way was forward and whether or not backward or sideways had some vital part to play, or had we just imagined it all?

Whether in a house or not, no one had read to me since I was a child. But there we were, finding it no waste of time, in a living room of kind chairs. We drank hot tea while Margie and Denis read short stories aloud. We watched a film and talked about it. We ate home-cooked food and slept on a bed in a room of memory. Outside, wild turkeys stenciled lawn snow with their steps. Inside, we prayed earthy prayers, drank unbittered coffee, and laughed a long hard while until the tears came. In between, we nestled into hours made for napping, writing, listening to music, or catching a firefly of thought day-glowing amid the sleepy afternoon. Such thoughts bid you to capture them and to marvel at what you hold.

While Jessica and I lingered with our day-glow clues to future paths, those who hosted us cut vegetables, spoke to neighbors, tried to figure out help for family illness and the unanswered questions of loved ones. Their ongoing earnest work in community allowed us individually to rest. Both the rest and the work that provided it offered the knowledge we sought.

If epistemology tells us how we know things, then Toad Hall and the House Between remind us that hospitality is a hard-fought-for epistemology. Scientific knowledge forges one crucial way of knowing and navigating the world. But a daily way of being offers its own sturdy truths.

In this, Margie glimpses something workable and wholesome about Jesus, for any who wonder who he might be. His way of being is to show hospitable welcome to any question we might have, any desire we hope to fulfill, and any closed door we wish to open. He labors at small, overlooked relational things to provide us such open spaces. Ask your question, and he'd often answer you by telling you a story.

"Why is locating God so difficult for us?" we might ask. Jesus answers with a tale about a sheep who wandered, a coin misplaced, two sons fragmented from family.

Margie's way imitates the master artist. Throughout the pages of this book, Margie gives voice to the many common questions we all ask. The big questions, such as, *What's the meaning of life? Where did I come from? What happens after death?* But also all the little questions that confront us daily. *You know that nightmarish feeling when you urgently need to reach someone and you can't?* A therapist asks, *So, why do you think you are here today?* A friend asks another: *What are you doing?* When knowingly provoking a lover, we ask ourselves, *Why do we enjoy doing this sort of thing?* A child asks, *Do animals go to heaven? Will I go to heaven when I die? Why did God make poison ivy?* A parent in exasperation asks, *How many times have I told you not to leave your stuff in the rain?* A parent having hurt their child asks, *How can I forgive myself?* Any of us ask ourselves, *Should I be ashamed to get help if I need it?*

With such questions in front of us, Margie tells a story and draws our questioning hearts back into the earthen world. We feel as though perhaps we are inhabiting the same world that God does and that our mundane interests are his and lovely. Margie's words have rabbit bones and finger blisters in them. Her sentences giggle. Syllables infuse our cups. It no longer seems irrational to ask. Can God, like a creaking floor, hold our night-lit weight?

As Jessica and I tried to step, Margie and Denis drew out a few dripping questions from their listening well. Their questions watered our talk and performed their nourishing work long after Jessica and I came home to our unnamed house.

Who knew that honest questions, earnest desires, and aching pains could find kind relief while eating toast, using a stenciled bathroom, washing a dish?

Margie tells her stories with words stained by spilled paint on a garage floor. She does not ask us to escape our world to find answers for what bothers or enthralls us. Instead, she raises the marvelous question: What if God likes to reveal his wonders at a table of companions, not far from a picture window in one direction and toilet paper in the other?

Zack Eswine, author of *Sensing Jesus: Life and Ministry as a Human Being*

PROLOGUE

"What is God doing in the sink?"

My granddaughter, Ava Lou, was standing on a stool washing dishes with a sink full of cold water and high soapsuds as only a four-year-old can "wash" dishes. She was looking at bobblehead Jesus, who was sitting on the kitchen windowsill overseeing the process at Toad Hall.

I wondered how to explain irony to her. How to say it had an obscure, but special meaning to me. I've often thought I should put it away because people must look at it and wonder if I'm a heretic of some kind, worshiping saints or idols or something equally suspicious. This is my explanation. He was a gift from a friend, Jeremy Huggins. Together we appreciate the humor and irony in Christian paraphernalia that's marketed in certain stores. Things like Frisbees that say "Flying High for Jesus." Or nightlights with the inscription, "Jesus is the light of the world."

So there Jesus sits, bobbling on the edge of my sink as a reminder to laugh at ourselves for the absurd ways in which we represent Christian faith to the world, and to try and push against the trivialization of such great a thing as the gospel. I mean no disrespect for a God I love. I think he knows that.

When it took too long to think of a simple answer to this dear child, she moved on to the next question. "Can I give God a bath? He wants a bath." I gently said, "No. He'll get all rusty inside and not bobble anymore." I quickly moved to pack him in a box, ready for my next kitchen. Yes, my next kitchen. The words were both exhilarating and terrifying.

Ava Lou and Micah, my daughter-in-law, were visiting for three days to help us clean out Toad Hall's attic. Micah's presence and help was stabilizing. I was thankful she was a marathon runner because there must have been a million trips up and down two flights of stairs. It was accomplished in record time because I was determined to be ruthless. Everything down and out. Throw away, give to family, give to charity, sell if possible. Label what to keep and where it should go in the next place. Done!

When we arrived at this house thirty-three years ago, our children were awestruck when we pulled up to the curb for the very first time and looked up at our new home. Our oldest daughter, who had just turned twelve, exclaimed, "Why, this must be exactly like Toad Hall!" They had never seen such imposing three-story homes with dormers and enormous front porches. They had only known low, one-story adobes that rambled along in the hot New Mexico sun. To them, an American Gothic Foursquare looked amazingly like a mansion, possibly even as great a house as Toad Hall from *The Wind in the Willows.* So that's what it became. Christened by our children: "Toad Hall."

In 1982, the following year, we began a ministry called Ransom Fellowship. It became my job to write updates to the friends and donors on our mailing list. It seemed appropriate to call the newsletter *Notes From Toad Hall.* I wanted it to be informative, but not so dull you'd want your time back after you read it.

The challenge was how to write truthfully about the place where we all must dwell in whatever is our ordinary and everyday. I didn't want to over-emphasize victorious Christian living, which can have a ring of falseness, or what our culture, Christians included, defines as success. The rhythm of ordinary life is rarely that exciting or sensational for any of us. I wanted to honestly share what it meant to be a faithful follower of Jesus, not so much when a hundred people praise your lecture on children's literature or how many times your husband is the main speaker at a prestigious conference. That part's easy. It has always been more difficult to honestly describe that ordinary place where God calls us to be faithful. The very place where the thistles and thorns of the fallen world creep into our vocations and callings every day. It's a place where there are painful disagreements with your spouse, where a child's vomit stains the woodwork, and where the espresso machine explodes. Faithfulness is tested and strained through the mundane, often boring offices of life where the pantry must be kept stocked and mistakes are made when filing your taxes. These things are so ordinary it's easy to forget this is where God mentors us and gives us grace. And rest. And meaning. And life. These were the bones that grew into a personal essay I included in every letter.

This is a collection of those essays from *Notes from Toad Hall.* They have been gathered together from the beginning of our sojourn back in 1981 until we left in 2014. I hope and pray that others might be as encouraged, as I have been, to recognize God's presence in the ordinary circumstances of our lives.

Life continues to be a demonstration of God in the sink with us. He has been with us through all stages of life, appearing in the unexpected joys of fireflies in summer and snowmen in winter, and mixing it up with the human struggles common to us all. And now, Jesus watches over us in the midst of boxes and the screech of packing tape, helping us move on to a new stage after so many years in one place.

There were reasons we moved from this hundred-year-old Midwestern home. We needed to leave before the decision was made for us. All our bedrooms were on the second floor. There was only a half-bath on the main floor. Our neighborhood was increasing in noise and traffic. As writers, we value quiet. With many of our closest friends having moved away, there was less community for us. We knew the longer we stayed, the harder it would be to say goodbye to a place where we lived more than half our lives. Frankly, old people can get calcified and stubborn.

Bobblehead Jesus watching over the sink.

We've been in our new home for a month, and today I'm sitting in my office looking out the window. About five feet away a little flycatcher hops down an oak limb looking for insects. The sun sends rays through the canopy into the ravine below. It lights leafy corridors with a hundred hues of green and gold. We are 85 percent moved in. Denis says it's 85 percent. I don't know why 85. I do know there are fewer boxes stacked in the living room. The ones that remain will wait as I slowly find new spaces for their contents.

Bobblehead Jesus has a new sink to oversee. God made it to our new home. As if I didn't think he would come? Each morning as I reach into the cabinet and pull out my coffee mug, I'm reminded that just as he watched over Toad Hall every moment of my life down through the years, he will bless this place, The House Between, and the people who dwell here as only he can.

THUNDERSTORMS AND ANGELS

SUMMER 1981

Everything we owned was strewn throughout the first and second floors of the house. Boxes teetered in stacks halfway to the ten foot ceilings; black plastic garbage bags spilled pillows and blankets; paintings and artwork wrapped in old sheets were stacked on radiators. The three people we knew in Rochester who had helped unload the truck were gone. The rental truck has been returned; we were all alone in our new home.

Our beds weren't set up, but I was determined to find clean pajamas for the kids among the litter of the bedrooms. Despite having carefully labeled every box we packed in Albuquerque, I gave up that search and began digging through stuffed animals, clothing, and blankets. Now all I wanted was a bath towel so I could shower. Everyone was crabby and starving. I waded through wads of newspaper on the kitchen floor. It was past suppertime and I now understood why spider mothers eat their young. At one time there had been food in our cooler, but three days of travel made what was left so revolting only a raccoon would have been interested.

In the sky to the southwest, purple-black clouds with a greenish tinge were mounting over St. Mary's hospital, and the giant elm trees lining the boulevards were unnaturally still. In the oppressive heat not a leaf turned. We felt faint rumbles like a distant war was being fought just beyond the horizon. No one wanted to stay home alone in a strange house with an attic door just off the upstairs hall and a basement with a cistern while Mother went in search of food. Staying together seemed wise.

After what seemed like days of carrot sticks and apple slices, Denis wanted meat. We thought we had seen a cheap steakhouse nearby, but we couldn't remember where. With Jerem and Sember crying with exhaustion and Marsena trying not to, we piled into our Volkswagen van. After a fruitless search for a restaurant, we finally stopped at a pay phone to see if we could find an address in a phone book. We were too tired to remember the names of any cheap steakhouses we had ever known. Anywhere. Anywhere on the continent. Or the world. We could only think of "Sirloin Stockade," but the restaurant pages were all torn from the book, and I was beginning to tear up, too.

Out of sheer desperation, Denis dialed "0." This was back when phone companies and information personnel were live and local. A telephone operator actually came on the line to ask how she could help. Denis explained we had just moved to Rochester, and didn't know where anything was, and was there a Sirloin Stockade or something like it nearby? Just an address would help. She first asked where we were. Not understanding, Denis said, "Rochester, Minnesota."

"No," she repeated, "where are you, as in what street are you standing on?"

Denis climbed back in the van, a wide grin on his face. She had not only told him which restaurant we should try, she had told him exactly how to get there, and informed him it was about three blocks from where he was standing. We were stunned. Could she be an angel? We had never heard of such a thing as a telephone operator giving that much help.

Marsena asked why I was crying. I felt relieved and couldn't stop saying, "Thank you God, thank you God, we were hungry, and so tired, and you sent a telephone operator to help us!"

By the time we got back to our new home, it was storming. Rain sheeted the windows and torrents of water swirled through the streets. No one wanted to sleep alone in a strange, new house. No way was Jerem going to lie down in a room stacked with shadowy boxes and lumpy shapes ready to spring to life in the dark. He always had an active nighttime imagination. We finally found sheets and blankets, shoved aside boxes in the largest bedroom, and made beds on the floor. We had just arranged our bodies and turned off the light when a flash so intense it momentarily blinded us as it lit the room. There was no time to count "Mississippi one, Mississippi two" to estimate how far away the lightning struck. The instantaneous concussion crashed through our chests and shook the house to its stone foundation. It was worthy of the 101st Airborne dropping a thousand bombs. In the darkness that followed we laughed nervously as we heard the howling of the civil defense sirens, first from the west and then from the north as they went off all over town.

Cuddling together, we prayed, thanking God for a dry home, kind people who helped us carry all our things inside before the rain, and a telephone operator who helped us find some supper. We had forgotten all about tornado weather rules, because we didn't even think of rushing our family to the safety of the basement.

The next morning sunlight sparkled through leaded glass windows as we found milk and cold cereal for breakfast. That's when the sirens began sounding again and again. We pulled a radio from a box, turned to a local station to see if there was some cause for alarm, and learned they were warning of flash flooding as the creeks and rivers overflowed their banks from the seven inches of rain that fell during the night—another reminder of how far we were from the high and dry deserts of New Mexico where seven inches of rain was almost the annual rainfall.

It didn't take long to unpack our belongings and settle into this solid, Gothic foursquare built in 1916. The amount of storage space in the garage, the dusty walk-up attic, and basement put me in a rapturous coma. Unbelievable, coming from a small home where every closet and shelf bulged! The honey-colored hardwood floors, the wide oak trim, and six panel doors gave the rooms a solidity that could surely withstand floods and tornados and soothe the worst family quarrels. Lovely touches here and there—high ceilings, leaded glass windows, and a screened-in back porch. I was in love.

There is no doubt Minnesotans have an accent. This was where I grew up, these are my people, but my ear could not hear it until I had lived in New Mexico for twelve years. I had forgotten how often they say, "Ya, sure," or end their sentences with a preposition. Now that I'm back, that sing-songy way of speaking and the elongated vowels slip easily off my native tongue, as if it had never left. I think we're home.

WHOSE CHILD IS THIS?

FALL 1987

Mother's Day was an improvement this year. I'm learning to appreciate breakfast in bed. Two years ago the technology of breakfast-making was simply beyond the skills of our two youngest, and they had sent up an uncooked egg rolling around the plate and a piece of burned toast without butter. This time they had everything in place—orange juice, boiled egg, buttered toast, a dollop of jam on the side, and a cup of tea just how I like. In fact, it was so fine I wrangled two more breakfasts that week by holding some of their precious belongings hostage until the following Saturday. It was just after bedtime when I had to run out to the backyard and put away bikes, soccer shin pads, sweatshirts, a paper route bag, two pairs of shoes, and a basketball. I was keeping most of it in my closet until I could think of an appropriate consequence for "How *many* times have I told you not to leave your stuff in the rain?" It seemed breakfast in bed would please them and mollify me.

A new car was another improvement. It came at just the right time at the right price. This one has air conditioning, but more importantly it has a heater, which our Volkswagen camper van did not have, having been purchased in New Mexico. Before buying the new car we had to sell the van.

We were so cold last winter. You can't believe how miserable it is to climb into a vehicle frozen so hard the seats crack when you sit on them. Which brings up another issue. Whatever our children's faults in the future, we must not forget some of the most inadvisable, dangerous, insane things we've done as adults. One of them being: on a trip to the far north to visit my family in the middle of winter, we placed a lit kerosene heater behind the front seats of our Volkswagen to keep us warm. It worked, but at some cost. The moisture from combustion caused our windows to build up with frost so thick it was furry. While Denis drove—for seven hours—the passenger (me) scraped like mad to keep a tiny square clear so the driver could see the road. So, yes. We need to remember this when our adult children do something *we* would never do, because we are responsible, sane, and have never imperiled the lives of our children.

We managed to sell the van. Which I can hardly believe since Jerem and Sember were "assisting" with the sale. I was watching from the kitchen window, clutching my throat, and praying as a potential buyer inspected it. Sember followed Denis and the potential buyer inside the van and helpfully pointed out the broken struts that hold the pop-up tent down. Those weren't *absolutely* essential, unless we were on the highway and met a truck. The vacuum it created could suck the top enough to pop it up, so the driver would shout *"Semi!"* whenever a truck approached. One of the backseat kids would jump up and hang on the handle to hold it down. They actually fought for the privilege, but I didn't think the man needed to hear about this.

When they started the engine and pulled away for a test drive, Jerem ran alongside shouting, "HEY, DAD! THERE'S SMOKE POURING OUT THE BACK!" The man bought it anyway, and all I could think was that God is surely with us even and in spite of our children.

Not long ago we had a death in our house—or, more accurately, a murder. Sember's dear gerbil, Muffin, escaped her cage during the night and went missing. She did this by repeatedly jumping straight up and hitting the top until she dislodged it. We thought it had been battened down tight enough to stop this from happening, but a thorough search the next day turned up some discouraging evidence. On the stair landing I found what at first looked like pieces of gray string. We didn't like to think it, but they gave off a suspicious odor and on closer inspection looked a bit like miniature intestines. Then under the chair in the living room, we found a tail and a tiny gerbil paw. Sasha had a smug look on her face as she sat on the back of the couch, fastidiously cleaning her face. Cats try hard to pretend they're not barbarians.

I felt honesty would be best for Sember. A head-on approach, no glossing over this death, might also be safer for any gerbil she might own in the future. I sat her down and told her what I'd found.

Her reaction followed a condensed version of Kübler-Ross' five classic stages of dealing with death. First, she denied it. "That can't be Muffin's tail! Maybe a wild mouse got into the house. We have to keep looking for Muffin." Then she was so angry with Sasha she wanted to kill her. When she gave that up, she sat on the couch and grieved with great heaving sobs. An hour later she rose, wiped her eyes, fetched her savings, and asked how much a new gerbil would cost.

Kübler-Ross would be proud.

I marvel at how many ordinary events provide a natural, completely spontaneous time for teaching children truths about life and God. Here it was for us that day: Death and Resurrection. Questions that led from *Do animals go to heaven?* to *Will I go to heaven when I die?*

It is a particular joy to be mother to three children, and I doubt my life shall ever be so intimately or constantly connected with three people who are so open to discuss the important questions of life. That is, if I'm alert enough to catch them at the right time.

At supper that evening, Sember's spontaneous outburst almost made me cry. With her face glowing, she said, "This has been such a great day. We rode our bikes to the library for some books, with my own money I bought a new gerbil I named Rosa, we're having pizza for supper, and after that we get to watch two cartoons." Some days are amazing.

This same daughter, who is just nine, began a counseling service in the basement where she sees people with problems: drug addicts, the homeless, bed-wetters, and those who want to become Christians. She gives them instructions:

* Be at my house at 9:00 p.m. every day for three years and I will check your blood for drugs.
* If you wet the bed, don't sleep with anyone.
* Use a plastic sheet with a lot of towels on top, and don't worry!

Sember's best friend Niki, six, has been hired to be her assistant because "as a mother of three whose husband has left her, she has nowhere to go and only twenty dollars to her name!" Sember reports: "These people need God and they need to be taught how to think!"

We agree, my daughter and I. When it comes to living everyday life, even I need help knowing how to think. I consider my main struggle the past few months: I am always behind. When I'm reasonably caught up, I still *feel* behind. I complicate this by becoming angry with myself for feeling behind even if I am not. Do you understand this?

I'm convinced there will always be scores of demands on our lives no matter what our age or stage of life. Just now I have an issue of *Notes From Toad Hall* to prepare, a dress to sew for Marsena's prom, a book to review, phone calls to make for Sember's third grade class, guests coming every day this week for discussions over meals or group studies, a banner to sew for church, and work on Jerem's science fair project, "Sweat and Soap." (I hate science fair projects, because they put as much pressure on the parent as they do on the student.) Meanwhile, Jerem is begging for more pets in addition to his gerbil and a chameleon even though I must check on these pets *every* day and remind him *every* day "it's been two weeks since you bought crickets and the chameleon is looking thin and grim."

Sunday I decided to take some time off. Denis can make waffles for lunch. He has perfected them—buttery, tender-crisp squares that hold rivers of golden maple syrup. The kids can do the dishes. For something completely other and completely relaxing, I stenciled the bathroom. Every square inch of it. The pattern pleasantly assaults you like an enormous peasant dress.

As I tap, tap, tapped the stencil brush thousands of times, I thought back to foundational principles. I resent my need to do that. To me, maturity ought to be moving forward, never back. I reviewed anyway:

* No one will die if I don't manage to complete everything. Someone may be a little disappointed, but they'll recover.
* Missing deadlines isn't always a question of failure—it only *feels* that way.
* There are only twenty-four hours in a day and I need seven of them to sleep (*eight*, Denis says).
* God made humans finite and after he made them, he said it was *good*.

It may be troubling to discover we can't do everything, be everywhere, know everything—as in "Where's the five dollars I left *right* here, Mom?" But there is comfort in accepting the limits God has placed on us and in knowing what we're called to do in this moment, at this point in life.

I remind myself that time spent listening and talking with my children may seem insignificant to others, but it is a gift to both of us. Especially when you find treasure in the midst of bickering and nonsense. Nothing compares.

By midnight Sunday, reviewing these things had settled my heart. God continues his long work, slowly renewing, perfecting my mind. The stenciling was complete and the pattern of vines and flowers trailing across the walls calmed my heart. I was putting away the paints when Denis walked in. He exclaimed over the new look and proclaimed it would make our house more marketable if we sell. Ha. I'm not that naïve. I know stenciling is about as appealing to some as pink tulips on black velvet wallpaper are to me.

Some weeks later, Sember, who is still our resident therapist, and I were the only ones home, sitting down together for supper. This gave her a chance to counsel me. She asked, "Do you have any problems you would like to ask me about? I could probably help you."

Trying to take her seriously and making an effort to be honest, I told her that very evening I was leading a Bible study Denis normally leads and I was nervous. I worried someone might ask me a question I didn't know how to answer, and I thought all who attended were probably a lot smarter than I was. It could be embarrassing.

She leaned forward (I like her technique) and earnestly promised that what she did in those situations always worked: "When someone asks me something I don't know, I look at them like they are crazy and say, 'WHAT?' Or, I just ignore them like they didn't say anything. They usually go away."

I stifled a laugh. "Hmmm, I don't know if that would work for a Bible study. I don't really want them to go away." Upon reflection, she thought maybe it wouldn't be such a good idea to use that technique on friends.

Her next suggestion was better: "I know! Just tell them you don't know and next week Dad will be back and they can ask *him!*"

With that settled, she pointed out I ought to write down her advice so I wouldn't forget. She even kindly offered to write it down for me. I assured her I could remember, but she made me repeat it one more time to make sure I got it right.

She prayed with me and, indeed, the study went very well.

When Denis travels, things often go awry at home, and that is when we miss him most. I surely wished he'd been home when I struck Sember. It was an honest accident, but what followed was not my best example of how to parent. I wished he was around, so he could say, "Awww, it could have happened to anyone, even me."

It was Sunday afternoon and our three kids and I went for a bike ride. We wanted to swim at the Y, but it was closed when we got there, so we turned back home. The first intersection we came to was a four-way stop with traffic coming from every direction. Sember became confused about whose turn was next and in fear of oncoming traffic, she suddenly turned her bike into my path and I collided with her and ran over her foot. We quickly dragged our bikes off the road and helped Sember to the side. She sat on the curb crying and holding her foot. The crying went on and on for the longest time and, being the miserable person I am, I told her to *stop* because I couldn't see anything wrong with it. I forced her to get on her bike and ride home. She made it, but cried most of the way.

Perhaps, like me, other mothers grow immune to their children's howls and death throes over mere scratches. We are predictably conditioned to ignore some life-threatening injury or disease. It's just a matter of when. This was my "when."

The next morning, her foot was swollen and she couldn't walk, so I took her to the doctor who examined and X-rayed it. He came back into the exam room with the tests, threw the X-ray onto the monitor, looked at me suspiciously, then said, "You didn't *know* it could have been broken?" After he cast it for three (three!) fractures, I was the one crying. I took her to Wendy's for lunch, and begged her to forgive me. She did so immediately, without reservation. I was stunned by her grace. By the forgiveness I received in that moment.

There are so many ways to fail as a mother and I've probably committed most of them. I don't nag very much. The trouble is when I do, it's concentrated to a near lethal dose. I did it to Jerem the other day. He is such a well-intentioned, happy person that to him, it's doubly shocking when he's attacked. It had to do with him recklessly spending all his allowance money without regard for his chameleon, who needs one lousy, fifteen-cent cricket per week to survive. And which pet he wanted desperately and swore always to love and to feed, and which pet was now gasping with starvation. All this illogically led to a lengthy recounting of grievances I had stored up against him. I raved on about the crummy way he leaves tools all over the yard to rust in the rain, the muddy sock balls left at the back door, the newspapers from his route strewn about the garage, etc., etc., etc. In a fury I gave him a quarter and sent him to the store for some crickets.

It took about fifteen seconds of silence after he quietly left for the echoes of my harangue to return to me. What a wretch, an absolute wretch I am. I knew I had devastated him with this uncontrolled attack. I ran to the garage to see if I could catch him before he rode off on his bike. I found him crouched in the corner, his head in his hands, crying. How could I mend it? (Not that he shouldn't learn to be responsible.) I owed him an enormous apology for unloading on him like that. How could I forgive myself as he forgave me?

There are times when I am sorry to be me. If I had not known what Paul said about himself—"What a wretched man I am! Who will rescue me from this body of death"—and if I had not known his answer— "Thanks be to God, through Jesus Christ our Lord!"—I would give up altogether (Rom. 7:24–25). Thanks to my children who have taught me much about spiritual growth.

Again and again we pick ourselves up. The process of confession and receiving forgiveness goes on and on to the end of life, or until Jesus returns and we are remade to be like him forever.

THE CASE OF THE MISSING BINOCULARS

WINTER 1987

Historically, I think the most sorrowful prayer for deliverance must have been spoken by Jesus as he prayed in the garden on the eve of his arrest: "O my Father, if it be possible, let this cup pass from me; nevertheless, not as I will, but yours be done" (Matt. 26:39 ESV). Following the example of the psalmist and many fathers and mothers from history, we cry out with our own prayers for deliverance. We pray for things large and small and don't always know whether this cup will "pass from me," or with God's help will I need to drink it?

Sometimes God grants answers to our prayers in the most singular way, like in the case of our son Jerem. I would like to say he was lucky, but since I'm mostly a Calvinist, I better say it was God.

It seems that God pays special attention to the hearts of children, kindly hearing them and pouring grace on them. I've known quite a few who have prayed a childish prayer and been answered in such a miraculous way it became evidence pointing toward the existence of God, rather like looking at the stars in the night sky and thinking there *must* be a creator.

There was a boy I knew in junior high, who hasn't made a profession of faith so far as I know. I've heard he concedes there is a God though he's not interested in him right now. He remembers when he was a little boy how much he loved butterflies, animals, and flowers. (He grew up to become a veterinarian.) Most of all he loved birds: how they flew, gracefully swooping from barn roof to the ground, how their songs carried across the land, how their colors flashed through the leaves. One warm day as he walked along a field of sweet clover on his dad's farm, he watched the tiny goldfinches dipping along the fence line and stopping to feed on thistle heads. He longed to hold one of these exquisite little birds. So he prayed aloud, "God, if there is a God, you could make a bird sit on my hand, and I will believe in you." He no sooner said the words and held out his hand when a bright yellow goldfinch perched on his finger and sang to him.

On the day I am remembering, Jerem's prayer was a prayer for deliverance from me: "God, please rescue me from my mom's anger. Please, please help me find those binoculars."

What precipitated this was that I noticed Denis' binoculars—a birthday gift from me—were missing. I knew right well who'd taken them and went straight to Jerem, who did not have permission to play with them. When confronted, he looked from side to side as only an eleven-year-old can and, seeing no escape, admitted he had "borrowed" them and forgotten where he left them.

His forgetting was, of course, no surprise. Many of us cannot remember where our coat is five minutes after it's shed. In fact, last Monday morning at bus time, when it was twenty degrees outside, after searching high and low for his coat, Jerem remembered he had forgotten that very item at his uncle's house. The problem is that his uncle lives four hundred miles north of us. We had been there for the weekend and weren't going back anytime soon.

I threatened to tell Denis that the binoculars were missing unless he found them within twenty-four hours. Yes. "I'm going to tell your father" is a shabby mother trick. I am that mean, but I like to excuse myself when I'm busy, tired, or hungry, which is most of the time. Jerem searched everywhere. He consulted his friends with whom he plays hunting, spying, and soldiering games. No luck. No one remembered. He went to bed sober and depressed that night. His last prayer before sleep was: "Dear God, please help me find those binoculars, because I can't remember where I left them."

That night he had a dream and relived what he was doing the last time he played with them. He saw himself in our walk-up attic where he and his friend Luke had been using them to spy on the neighbor. He had wrapped them in an old blanket to protect them and placed them behind some dusty boxes under the eaves for safekeeping. Sensing God's presence as only a child can, he woke up that very moment, knowing exactly where they were. He turned on the light and wrote himself a note as a reminder. In the morning, he found the binoculars just as the dream had revealed. We never in a hundred years would have found them. He retrieved them and, handing them over to me beaming and triumphant, said, "God *answered* my prayer!"

Indeed, God delivers us in many ways and gives us good gifts in his own perfect time. He hears the prayers and pleas of his children. There are times when I can't think why he has gifted me—a sometimes crabby, impatient mother—with eternal life.

TRASH, KIDS, AND SNAKES

SUMMER 1990

Last winter I bought a small trailer for not much money. As they say in Minnesota, it was not too baduva deal. It's good for hauling furniture, large Christmas trees, trash, and all sorts of junk. I also knew it would come in handy when we cleaned out our attic, basement, and garage. That day came this spring.

Jerem, Sember, and I began the process. We hauled to the garage canning jars, old carpets, kerosene heaters, a broken black-and-white TV set, old doors, scrap lumber, broken suitcases, and twenty-seven metal venetian blinds. That was only the beginning. We still had about one hundred square yards of cardboard boxes full of plastic peanuts sitting in the attic. Don't ask. The garage was bursting but we'd put the trailer to good use when Denis got home from his last trip.

Denis took one look around and turned a shade of gray. The garage wasn't just a mess of my junk collections—our kids had contributed to the chaos with stacks of undelivered newspapers, old bike parts, and worn out sports equipment. As he began throwing things in the trailer, I suggested we'd better think the whole thing through. In other words, how were we going to organize? He paused, hands on hips. "Why would you organize trash?"

I took a breath and explained that I had called the County Recycling Center and each trailer load would cost us $12.75. That's if it contained metal, burnables such as wood, and plastic, but if the load did not contain all of one type of trash, we'd have to sort it out there, and since they recycled cardboard, we didn't have to pay for that or newspapers, but on the other hand, they would pay us for glass and aluminum. So we may as well sort here.

Denis scowled and began throwing old lumber on top of the cardboard in the trailer. "Just a minute!" I cried. "We don't want to mix up that space. Since they charge us for wood—why put in cardboard? Unless we have a whole trailer full of wood and make a separate trip?"

"So just *how* do you want me to do this?" Denis asked. I proposed we could do it however he decided was best since he now had all the facts.

We stood quietly awaiting his decision, except for Sember who was sweeping up choking clouds of dust from the floor. The minutes dragged on while Denis looked more and more irritated. I thought, *Oh, yes. A typical Haack Family Work Day. So much fun.* I began rolling my eyes a little. Not a lot. Just quiet little rolls. But Denis didn't miss that small movement.

Finally, Denis emptied the cardboard from the trailer. "We'll fill it with the other stuff first."

He picked up a heavy box of old paint cans to heave in and I yelled, "No! Not *that!* Sorry, I forgot to mention. Hazardous waste. That can't be mixed in with the anything else. They only accept that on Saturday mornings between eight and noon. And one other thing: they'll take the old tires, but that'll cost us extra."

Dropping the box with a crash, eyes bulging slightly, he picked up a plastic bag full of grass clippings and plants. I so hated to say, but I had to tell him he was holding compostable material and that couldn't be mixed in with anything else, either. However, we could get rid of it for free if we hauled it to the city's compost pile.

By then I was beginning to wonder why someone as intelligent as my husband could not organize a few little trips to the dump. I became irritated myself and more than a little impatient. Now Denis was snapping at us, Jerem was heaving big meaningful sighs, and Sember continued on obliviously. (Every family needs someone like her. She is a wonderful antidote for family tension. As long as she was able to focus, she could forge ahead with good humor, ignoring the stress around her, humming merrily as she worked.)

My philosophy of work is similar to that of the seven dwarves in Disney's *Snow White*. You remember how they got their jobs done? Quickly! No complaining! In no time at all with cooperation, smiles, willing hands, all the while singing "Whistle While You Work." Ha ha. I know this isn't reality any more now than it was back in the Depression when that movie was made. Still it's my inherent weakness to expect it from my family.

That afternoon I was reminded of another reason family projects often don't work around here. I had lately been contemplating a phrase from 1 Corinthians 13:5 *Love is not easily provoked.* Not easily provoked. Case in point. I *am* easily provoked. Guess who provokes me most easily? Denis. The person I love most in the world, am most committed to. He provokes me. Most of the time over some small thing.

I was convicted by my lack of patience—my failure to see, through his eyes, the chaotic, complicated mess we had created in the garage. I was convicted by my surly response to his stress, not that he couldn't have used some extra patience of his own. What was more distressing was the speed at which I can move from eager-beaver work projects to door-slamming, box-kicking anger.

Love is patient. Love is kind. *Love is not easily provoked.* It stays calm. It explains patiently. Love might even consider the stress of re-entering the family dynamic after you've been on the road for days at a time and haven't had time to recover. It also considers the impact of the smallest eye-roll.

There is no way I can do this. The only chance I have for changing is if God helps me carry my burdens inch by painful inch.

It took longer than I had planned, but we finally got the loads hauled to the Recycling Center in my handy little trailer. With a clean garage, we were ready for summer.

After three years of drought, spring rains have been heavy and welcome this year. They deeply drench the lawn, soak the trees, and cause our tulips to blaze. The snakes must have appreciated the rains because they hatched in greater numbers.

On a sunny warm day, Sember found a long, green garter snake in our front yard and screamed for me to come. They are harmless. Apart from the few timber rattlers that live in the river bluffs, we have only harmless snakes in Minnesota. I grabbed it by the tail and we watched, fascinated while it made esses in the air.

It was the sort of thing that brought back memories. On laundry day, my brother and I sometimes collected a basketful of garter snakes. Holding the lid down tight, we took them out one by one and pinned them to the clothesline amid the white sheets that billowed in the sun. We hid behind an old stock tank and watched as our unsuspecting mother came out to gather the dry linens. Her shrieks of surprise delighted us as unpinned snakes fell writhing into her clothesbasket. She was hard to scare and probably faked it for our sakes.

Sember and I decided the snake had too much potential to pass up. What fun to surprise someone with a snake! We waited until Jerem came home from school and headed for the bathroom. Our bathrooms don't have locks on the doors: we never bothered to install them because our policy is to not disturb anyone's privacy when the door is closed. Sember and I slipped quietly up the stairs, slowly cracked the door, and released the writhing reptile. We were rewarded by loud shrieks and thumps that told us he was jumping into the tub. Fortunately, Jerem is a pretty good sport and decided immediately he ought to pass this favor on to his dad, who was speaking at a conference in New Jersey at the time.

Denis has such a phobia of snakes, I hesitated to let Jerem release it in our bed like he wanted, or even to drop it on his lap as he read the newspaper. I was truly afraid he might have a heart attack. Anyway, it was all for nothing, because we forgot to hide the snake's cage and the normally unobservant Denis walked in the door from the airport and spotted it instantly. Jerem simply waved it in Denis' face, which was almost as good as releasing it in the bathroom.

Perhaps my favorite response was when Sember greeted her friend Rachel in the backyard. All she did was hold its weaving body with its red tongue flicking her in the face and Rachel bent double and screamed for five excruciating minutes. This is no exaggeration. Neighbors ran to their windows and workmen in the neighborhood paused to look in our backyard to see if someone had died.

Why do we enjoy doing this sort of thing? It seems that not only am I easily provoked, I enjoy provoking others, or at least scaring them. It may take some time to become more sensitive about crossing the line from okay joking to provoking.

Not long ago, I ran out of energy before my daily work was done. Jerem came home from school and saw me lying on the couch amid piles of laundry. He took one look, pivoted on his heel, and was gone. He was soon back, leading Denis from the office. Jerem announced I was not to move—he and Dad were going to fix dinner. Jerem had even planned the menu.

Deeply touched, I whispered, "Jerem, this is so kind of you. You don't know how much I appreciate this."

"Aw, it's okay, Mom," he responded. "One look at you and I knew that if we were going to have any dinner at all, I'd have to fix it myself. And I happen to be very hungry."

I sank back. So much for altruistic motives. I laughed at the irony because, obviously, there's plenty I do prompted by selfish motives—especially if I have an audience. It can be disheartening. It seems God desires us to keep going while at the same time being mindful of our condition. This is who we are: incomplete works, broken, in need of repair, but recipients of grace. In Ephesians 1:7–8, Paul says God has *lavished* grace on us. Lavish means extravagant—generously, completely, like toast buttered to the edge. Praise God, who observes as I terrify my child just so I can have a laugh, yet still pours his lavish grace upon me.

Our menu that night was very good. A bit light on the leafy greens, but I wasn't complaining about venison chops, Greek flatbread, corn, and Jell-O with whipped cream. No.

CONSIDER THIS

WINTER 1994

Eight hundred years before Christ was born, Isaiah prophesied that out of the tribe of Judah, from Jesse, the father of King David, would come a shoot. A descendant. He would be a root growing out of dry ground. In a landscape of death, the "Rose of Sharon" would grow. This descendant would be so splendid and so deeply rooted he would redeem men from their darkness and rescue creation from the fall. His might would extend not only to the great griefs and tragedies of all time, but to the everyday illnesses and trials of our lives. Meanwhile, we are still waiting for the consummation of this regeneration plan begun before the foundation of time and revealed in Bethlehem two thousand years ago. There is much about creation and humans and their troubles—some great, some small—that waits for redemption.

Consider poison ivy: a beautiful, waxy-green plant with dark leaves arranged in patterns of three. Without care or fertilizer, it can form a dense ground cover, stand as a single healthy plant, or even become a deeply rooted vine twisting up a tree. It produces attractive clusters of creamy white berries. In fall, it turns a beguiling red. It could look lovely in an arrangement or even a garden except for its toxic oils and the havoc it wreaks on human skin.

Why did God make it? No one wonders more than our son, Jerem, who regularly experiences this form of broken creation, if it is that. He rides a mountain bike with friends whenever he can, 180 miles per hour straight down the Mississippi River bluffs resplendent with poison ivy. It's inevitable that while hurtling down the slopes he'll wipe out in a luxurious patch and from these accidents, he'll contract a raving case of itching blisters. After his most recent wipeout, I heard a lot of scratching and complaining, until his uncle recommended a cure which Jerem followed to the letter.

A day or so later, a young doctor friend noticed the bright red, weeping condition of his legs and asked what happened. It looked like third-degree burns.

Jerem replied he was curing himself of poison ivy. "You should know this," he said, "in case you get a patient with poison ivy. You take a 3M pot scrubber, soak it in undiluted bleach, and use it to scratch until the blisters come right off! The poison ivy is gone!" Replaced with third-degree burns instead? Thanks, Uncle Dallas. Do not try this at home.

Our friend frowns on home remedies and suggested that a simple application of steroid cream might be more effective in countering the effects of the fall.

Consider something so small as a tooth: a bit of hard enamel, shielding the sensitive pulp, seated in bone, and used for grinding and tearing. Despite its size, there is nothing like the pain of a tooth to get your attention during the night hours, when you cry out to God and promise to leave off all your addictions if only he will stop your suffering. When it finally gets so bad you can no longer stand it, you call the dentist. You can be sure you'll need to pay hundreds of dollars for the attention.

My trouble was a broken molar. It started last June and to this day it still hurts. I wonder why we just didn't pull it out and be done with it. (Another home remedy?)

In August I finally got it capped with gold. Why gold? Because "it might need a root canal and gold is easier to drill through." Okay.

When I returned for the final fitting, the dentist patiently tried to seat this new cap in the back of my mouth which was benumbed, wide-open, sheathed in plastic skirting, and bedecked with numerous sucking, spraying, and drilling instruments hanging from my lips. With each try, his gloves grew slipperier until he dropped the cap in the back of my throat. I was so alarmed, thinking I was going to inhale the thing and die right there, I half sat up and coughed hard. (My last name is not Haack for nothing.) The gold cap shot across the room, hit the wall, and skidded under a table.

We were all embarrassed. My dentist apologized profusely, cleaned it off, reached in my mouth, and dropped it again. That time I was ready for him: I simply closed my throat and stopped breathing.

Unbelievably, he did it a third time. He felt bad, but not bad enough to give his services free.

I went home to wait and things got worse. When I went back, sure enough, I needed to see an endodontist for a root canal. (I didn't know people were making a special living just by sucking out tooth nerves.) Suffice it to say that a small piece of enamel and dentin can ruin a vacation, create more pain than one thought possible, and be an excellent reminder that I need deliverance from this body, just to be rid of my teeth.

And lest you think I'm so silly as to believe redemption is only about weeds and broken teeth, consider relationships. How their sadness and grief often cause us to cry! Recently, Jerem, who is now a senior in high school and feeling the conflict between his growing independence and parental authority, left the house one day in a black funk. When he returned, he had a surprising and unusual request for us. He had run into a friend who'd been homeless for two weeks. (Reasons are private except to say that there's been trouble in his family's life.) Jerem wondered if we would consider letting him live with us. It was startling because we were under the impression that he thought no one would *want* to live with us—*if* they had a choice.

Despite already having two adolescents, which is more than enough at any time, we agreed to a trial period and possibly more. Perhaps God is drawing this young man to himself. Perhaps his way to regeneration lies through our living room and pantry. We pray so.

Finally, consider a toddler. My youngest nephew, Carson, is a child to melt any woman's heart. At just over a year, he looks innocent enough to eat butter and never have it melt in his mouth.

Carson has a peculiar trait—at least it's peculiar to me since I'm a woman. He doesn't like women. Oh, he likes his mother well enough and he tolerates his sisters, but he scorns all other females. Since he'll have nothing to do with us, we aunts have perversely enjoyed teasing him. He adores his daddy and is very pleasant with men and boys. There seems no reason for this other than it's just Carson being Carson.

One Sunday as I sat beside him during church, he quietly squirmed around on his father's lap and noticed I was sitting too close. My arms were crossed and I was concentrating on prayer when he scowled and slapped my hand. Startled, I looked up. His grinning father leaned over to me and whispered, "He needs to get saved."

Stifling my laughter, thought, *How true.* After all, even cute little Carson will need to be rescued from himself, like the rest of us. As babies, we are neither innocent nor perfect. Yet many parents are shocked to find they have actually passed their broken natures on to their children, even as the Bible says we will. David laments, "I was sinful at birth, sinful from the time my mother conceived me" (Ps. 51:5). We don't just grow into sin. It is in us from the beginning. Intrinsic. Genetic. Innate.

Some of my earliest memories from childhood are of things I purposely did. I knew were wrong. I try not to think too much about them. I believe by faith they truly are put away "as far as the east is from the west," like God says (Ps. 103:12). One day I will fully appreciate this as God intends.

Until then, I consider Jesus, that root of Jesse. "A shoot will come up from the stump of Jesse; from his roots a Branch will bear fruit" (Isa. 11:1). I have grown to love that shoot, that flower pushing up out of dry ground. Someday we will all be whole. I see it coming and with it "creation itself will be liberated from its bondage to decay and brought into the glorious freedom of the children of God" (Rom. 8:21).

This ancient carol by an anonymous German composer sings the beautiful message of Christmas—ever new, ever healing: when the infant Jesus returns as Christ the King, he will "dispel with glorious splendor / the darkness ev'ry where."

Lo, how a Rose e'er blooming
From tender stem hath sprung!
Of Jesse's lineage coming
As men of old have sung.
It came, a flowret bright,
Amid the cold of winter,
When half-spent was the night.

Isaiah 'twas foretold it,
The Rose I have in mind;
With Mary we behold it,
The virgin mother kind.
To show God's love a right
She bore to men a Savior,
When half-spent was the night.

This flow'r, whose fragrance tender
With sweetness fills the air,
Dispels with glorious splendor
The darkness ev'ry where.
True man, yet very God,
From sin and death He saves us
And lightens ev'ry load.[1]

PARENTING. I'M DONE

SPRING 1996

This year our youngest graduated from high school. This is one of the landmarks for parents, like getting the last baby out of diapers. Sember is done with high school and it's a relief to have some kinds of parenting over. No more micromanaging sleeping and waking patterns (as if I ever succeeded). No more nagging about a junk food, sugar-filled diet. She can pierce her navel, throw a rod in her car, or live in Mozambique if she wants. We will sympathize and advise. But our primary work as parents is done and now I'm going to sleep all night for the next ten years.

After twenty-six years of parenting, you'd think I could claim to be an expert on child-rearing and allow other parents to pay me for learning exactly how it's done. But it looks as if my only expertise may be noting the ironies and humor children bring to our lives. Running a close second is my remarkable ability to make unwanted suggestions and unenforceable rules. I have had to learn to hope in the grace and power of God. I think.

The attitude we've tried to achieve through the years is beautifully summarized by Covenant Seminary professors Dan Doriani and Jack Collins in a little leaflet called *Rearing Covenant Children In Faith.* They emphasize "parenting in confidence without presumption." That is, "confidence in the biblical promise that God loves and covenantally claims the children of believers." But, as they quickly add, this can be "misinterpreted as a guarantee that the children will be saved, if the parents carefully train them in the faith."[1]

Doriani and Collins affirm two truths:

First, the children of believers differ from other children in that they have the privileges of covenant upbringing. There is ground for confidence that the Lord sets them apart by placing his love on them. Second, we know that Adam literally raised Cain, that Isaac raised Esau, that David's favorite son betrayed him. Each had the privileges of the covenant but rejected the faith of their families.

While warnings forbid over-confidence, promises instill a humble confidence in God's covenantal provisions and inspire diligent obedience.

In our early years of parenting, we were plenty self-confident. We were certain that we would avoid all the mistakes our parents and friends had made, and that raising children was a snap if you just read the right books and paid attention to a few basic principles.

We had no idea what the grace of God delivered to us in the first bundle we brought home from the hospital. We loved her so much. She was the perfect baby. The perfect child—almost. We eventually discovered she had a few flaws, but overall, she was intelligent, sensitive, obedient, and compliant. We smugly believed we had shaped her ourselves. We were great parents, but probably anyone could do this if they just put their mind to it.

We had to wait six years for two more children whom God specially designed with side benefits that could address our delusion and teach us a little humility. What a wonder they were! Delightful. Normal. Naughty children. However, they didn't fit into the nice little box I had prepared for them. It seemed no matter what method I applied to raising these two, they tested my equilibrium in most areas of life. I couldn't seem to apply discipline with consistency. I lost patience. I didn't retain my old habits of prayer and Bible reading, which I believed were key to my spiritual and mental health. By just being children with their never-ending needs, their mischief and little rebellions, they easily poked holes in my resolve to be a better mother. I was always starting over.

Self-righteousness can put you at risk for a hard fall, so when I hit bottom, my confidence in child-rearing collapsed. I was disturbed by at least two things: first, by the Experts who promised everything would be perfectly okay if only I followed their advice. The second was having to face my own fallen nature—I had somehow passed it on to my sweet little munchkins. Almost every day they were a reminder of how unreasonable I could be.

I remember a day when a friend dropped off our order of fresh milk from the dairy. I was on the phone, so she set the two gallons of milk in glass jugs on the floor inside my front door.

Only that morning I had told the children that when they had accidents—like spilling their drink at the table, which happened every noon, like clockwork—I knew it was not because they were being disobedient. Therefore, I would not be upset with them. They listened with big eyes to another of Mom's turning over a new leaf.

Jerem was three at the time, and when he spotted those milk jugs, he decided: "Me hep, Mommy." With enormous effort, he picked them up and staggered toward me. I turned in time to see him trip, clink the bottles together, and send a tidal wave of milk and glass across the entry and down the carpeted hall. I screamed and burst into tears, and then I spanked him.

I was caught in moments like this when I saw myself with new eyes. I imagined our children one day sitting in a therapist's office and weeping, "My mother always…" or, "It was my father…" No matter how hard we try not to, we hurt our children. Usually it's unintentionally, but sometimes not! On this side of heaven there wasn't a snowball's chance in hell for me to raise perfect children because as a parent, I was so imperfect. The confidence with which I began parenting was replaced with a boatload of guilt. I needed forgiveness from both God and our children.

In the midst of learning we weren't such great parents after all, I really hoped the Experts would help us calm down and sort out the confusion surrounding child-rearing. It was unbelievable how many people out there claimed to know just what we needed. They had the exact solution (all of them different) for every problem you or your child might have.

We live at a time when Americans have grown accustomed to quick fixes that can be applied to any problem in life. As Christians, we can't escape these pressures from our culture. Many have come to believe that complex relationships can be explained by simple principles. So if you discover these principles and reduce them to a series of steps, you're assured of success. You can lose weight, invest finances, restore a broken marriage, and raise genius children if you faithfully apply their methods. Every few years, when someone discovers the secret to successful parenting, we who deeply desire our children to love and obey God and succeed in this life find it tempting to believe claims that guarantee success, especially when the material is reinforced with proof texts from the Bible.

The Christian marketplace is full of people who claim to have authoritative and comprehensive knowledge of godly parenting. They have devised techniques, steps-to-success, and principles for parenting. It's hard to miss these people if at any time in your life you've stepped into a Christian bookstore, attended Sunday school, or listened to Christian radio. As we sorted through the literature, it became clear that both parents and the Experts often seized upon "one principle and stressed it to the neglect of other parts of biblical truth about parenting" (Doriani & Collins).

For example, one child-growth psychologist, popular when Sember was a baby, insisted that her entire psyche would be formed by the time she was eighteen months old, and that if you failed to love and stimulate her in the proper way even from *conception*(!), she would suffer failure for the rest of her life. That form of determinism stole what little hope I had, and I wondered whether I should just kill myself or give the kids up for adoption.

Dr. Dobson's *Dare To Discipline* was the parents' bible when our children were babies. He certainly helped us have the courage to discipline our children, but my mistake was thinking that his suggestions and principles were equally applicable to all children. So, for example, when I instituted his chart and reward system for doing chores, I wasn't prepared for it to fail so miserably. It worked well for our oldest, who was compliant and took responsibility seriously. But Jerem didn't have a shred of interest in stickers and stars. As for Sember, she was only mildly interested in the chart for its artistic possibilities and often stole the stickers and put them up in everyone's columns just for the beauty of it. We found that an "undue emphasis on methods can decline into self-serving attempts simply to control a child" (Doriani & Collins).

We tried seminars. We went to a five-day conference where we learned how to solve all our family's spiritual problems if we followed the steps of action presented to us. At the time it seemed so right and so possible. But as the days went by and the predicted outcomes did not fall into place, we grew deeply discouraged. In the following months we began to understand the theological and practical problems with this approach. This was simply another form of determinism that reduced human behavior and relationships to a series of steps that, if followed exactly, are sure to produce a divinely ordained outcome.

Experts can be helpful, but their ideas must be thoughtfully examined. We should be cautious about listening to anyone who guarantees success or claims to have the final word on parenting. Legalism and self-righteousness are often a by-product of such books and programs. When parents adopt a program an Expert recommends, they can be tempted to criticize other parents for not doing the same, or to pontificate on why their child is having difficulties. Parents can also become smug when they compare their compliant children to someone else's child, who may not be so naturally complaint. Not all children are made that way.

However much we wish there were clear outcomes, Scripture does *not* give us step-by-step instructions for raising children with the complete assurance that they will enter adulthood as happy, healthy, productive believers. We have a proverb (*not* a promise) that gives us hope that if we "Train a child in the way he should go, and when he is old he will not turn from it." (Prov. 22:6). Scripture provides some principles. Maturity and experience supply some suggestions. But there is no God-authored manual with guarantees.

Notice the curious events surrounding Samson's birth (Judg. 13). His mother was barren when an angel came to tell her she was going to have a son, and that he was to be a Nazirite. His life work would be delivering Israel from the oppression of the Philistines. When she told her husband, Manoah, about this strange visitor, he prayed that God would send this person again "to teach us how to bring up the boy who is to be born" (v. 8). He must have been thinking of the awesome responsibility that had fallen on them. How they must have desired to do it exactly right!

The next time the angel showed up—theologians say there are reasons to believe this was the pre-incarnate Christ—he came again to Manoah's wife. (It's interesting that he came to the woman first both times. To receive such a serious message establishes her as an important and equal player in this scene.) When they asked him the big question, *What is to be the rule for the boy's life and work?*, what an opportunity this was for God to give us the final word on how to parent! I mean *really.* If you were the Holy Spirit, how could you pass up the perfect chance to outline God's Way for Raising Children?

The answer was basically, "Don't drink wine, don't eat unclean food, don't shave the boy's head, and do all I have commanded you." What? This has nothing to do with character!

Once again, God surprises us. What the angel told them was simply a repeat of what the Scriptures required concerning one who has taken the Nazirite vow. So the manual for raising successful children doesn't appear after all.

It's instructive to look further at Samson's life. He is at once amazing and tragic. A child who grew up and out of his parent's control—but never out of God's control. God used this very sinful and wonderful man, even in death. The account of his life in the book of Judges astounds me with its messiness. Betrayal, lies, revenge, violence, prostitutes, adultery, imprisonment, and torture. If this were our son, it would not ever be a story we would want to live through, nor would we want to tell it to others. And yet in Hebrews 11, Samson is counted among those of great faith. Who can fathom God's ways?

As a parent I also take courage from the story of Adam and Eve. God was their father. He placed them in a perfect environment. They had every opportunity to enjoy that privilege. God took such special care of them that he came every day to walk and talk with them in the garden. And yet if they, in such a setting, chose to disobey God and plunge all of mankind into sin, isn't there the possibility that, despite my best efforts, my own dear children will make sinful choices? Sure.

I want to raise my children in the faith and by faith as well as I can. In knowing God, I won't give up hope. I believe that according to his providence, all things are in his hands, including the lives of my children. And remember, the story is not over yet.

Comprehending a tiny fraction of this fills me with relief, and has sometimes allowed me to laugh at the ridiculous weight I placed on certain things. My mother raised six children and told me with authority that my children weren't as bad as I imagined and maybe I could lighten up a little.

This is what I'm talking about, for example. We live just beyond the one-mile boundary for our local high school which, according to their regulations, meant

Sember was going to have to walk to school every day for three years; she could not legally ride the bus. Secretly, we grinned and rubbed our hands. Walking! What good discipline this would be for her! We thought *now* she will have to get up at a *decent* hour each day in order to make it to school on time. However, as everyone knows, walking takes a terrible toll on the lives of teenagers. Most of the time this could be avoided if only parents were thoughtful enough to buy them a car or drive them every day.

A few days after school started, we watched dumbfounded as Sember stepped out of a school bus that stopped in front of our house. In the mornings, a bus would pull up to the corner and patiently wait as she calmly descended the stairs in her stocking feet, toast in one hand, paused on the porch to put on her shoes and, with the dignity of the Queen of England, strolled to the bus.

I was annoyed almost every morning. This was against the rules. Students were not allowed on a bus without a special picture ID issued by the district. I grilled her: "This is *not* a scheduled stop! You *don't* have an ID. You should be walking! You could *at least* not keep that poor bus driver waiting for you."

Every morning she patiently explained: "But the bus driver *likes* me and *he* doesn't mind, so why should you?"

Every morning, our neighbor across the street drank coffee on his porch, watched her and laughed at both of us. He said anyone that resourceful would be going places in this world.

He was right to laugh. I finally gave up my insane campaign to make her walk to school. On the last day of October 1995, we snapped a picture of Sember regally entering the bus, made the picture into a coffee mug, and gave it to our neighbor for Christmas with a thank you for helping us see a little more clearly and laugh a little more.

Margie and Sember . . . done parenting?

DEATH COMES FOR A BISHOP

SPRING 1997

Almighty and most merciful Father,
we have erred and strayed from
your ways like lost sheep;
we have followed too much the devices and
desires of our own hearts;
we have offended against your holy laws;
we have left undone those things which we
ought to have done, and
we have done those things which we
ought not to have done, and
there is no health in us.
But you, O Lord,
have mercy upon us miserable offenders;
spare those, O God, who confess their faults,
restore those who are penitent,
according to your promises declared unto
mankind in Christ Jesus our Lord.
And grant, most merciful Father, for his sake,
that we may ever hereafter live
a godly, righteous, and sober life,
to the glory of your holy Name.
Amen.[1]

Originally taken from the 1549 *Book of Common Prayer*, these words were written by Archbishop Thomas Cranmer, a man I have thought much about lately. At first, I was attracted to his creative way of putting things. That is no surprise since even secular historians admit his prayers, liturgy, and confessions have a quality of literary beauty, of excellence in English prose unsurpassed by anything before or since his time. Hillare Belloc writes:

> Thomas Cranmer, as anyone who will read the mere outstanding facts of his life can see, was many things that many men have been—a hypocrite, a time-server, a coward, a great scholar, timid and suave in manner, courteous also, an intriguer, and a quite successful layer of traps for the unfortunate. Yes, he was all this: but he was something more. He was a master of the word . . .[2]

He wasn't *only* "a master of the word"; Cranmer was a man with clay feet, but one who knew and loved God. His prayers pierce my heart. They turn me toward Christ with fresh desire and worship. When I read "there is no health in us," I know it to be true of me. All I do, my purest thoughts, my most selfless acts, are stained by shades of sin. My only hope is in Christ.

Thomas Cranmer served as ecclesiastical head of the church in England during the reign of King Henry VIII. It was a tumultuous time of transition and change for the Church. The king was no lover of the Reformation, which was going full tilt on the continent. It was for personal and political reasons that he chose to break with the Church of Rome and begin the Church of England. It was partly through Cranmer's influence that King Henry was convinced to issue a royal proclamation placing the first printed English Bible in every church in England for the public to freely read. It proved so popular with the people that the Bibles had to be chained to their tables to prevent them from being stolen.

When King Henry was on his death bed, he called for Cranmer. He had lain sick and dying for days while his physicians hovered about him. No one dared mention he was dying, because parliament had passed an act that upon pain of death no one should speak of the King's death. At last, one very brave Christian doctor came to the king and told him there was no hope for recovery. The doctor suggested he prepare himself for death and call upon God for grace and mercy as every Christian man ought to do. King Henry felt so weak and sick that the truth had to be acknowledged. As he reflected on his sins, which were many and great, he said, "Yet is the mercy of Christ able to pardon all my sins, though they were greater than they be." He sent for Cranmer to advise him in this spiritual matter.

By the time Cranmer arrived, the king was "speechless and almost senseless." He reached for Cranmer's hand and grasped it. The Archbishop of Canterbury exhorted him to put his trust in Christ, and asked him to give some sign that he trusted only in the Lord. The king wrung his hand with all his failing might. He died shortly after.

I have often despised this man—this king with six wives, who had put some of his wives away because they could not bear children, and who had executed the others. It is odd to think that he may be our brother, that he may live in Christ, that Cranmer may have helped him into the Kingdom.

Those were times of dreadful uncertainty. The political winds could blow any direction. Today in power and good favor. Tomorrow arrested and sent to the Tower of London. The next day released and your fortunes restored. The following day rearrested and your head in the basket.

In the years following King Henry's death, as the child King Edward VI ruled, Cranmer continued to advise the king as a member of the Privy Council.

King Edward was a good king, but very young. He ruled from age nine until he died at sixteen of consumption. It was after his death that Lady Jane Grey, with Cranmer's help, was put on the throne as a Protestant queen. She reigned for ten short days until King Henry's daughter, Mary, stormed into power. She was a devout Catholic and her first act was to restore the Church of Rome. The Catholic bishops returned to power in England, and many Protestants, especially leaders who had been influenced by the Reformation in Europe, were imprisoned, beheaded, or burned at the stake. During her four-year reign, more people were put to death, driven into exile, imprisoned, and tortured for their religious beliefs than in any other period of English history. Thus Mary became known as "Bloody Mary."

Over the years, Cranmer became more thoroughly Protestant in his beliefs. He had written much of *The Book of Common Prayer*. His work was greatly influenced and based on the writings of the early church fathers including Augustine. *The Book of Common Prayer* became widely read and its truths were impressed on the hearts of the people. Belloc writes: "He [Cranmer] provided a substitute for the noble Latin rhythms on which the soul of Europe had been formed for more than a thousand years, and he gave to the Church of England a treasure by the aesthetic effect of which more than by anything else her spirit has remained alive . . ."[3] It was more than an "aesthetic effect." It was the power of the Holy Spirit at work in a man who understood the redemptive work of the cross that had been hidden in the rituals and the corruption of the Church for years.

Almighty God, our heavenly Father,
who of your tender mercy did give your
only Son Jesus Christ to suffer death
upon the Cross for our redemption;
who made there
(by his one oblation of himself once offered)
a full, perfect and sufficient sacrifice, oblation,
and satisfaction for the sins of the whole world;
and did institute, and in his holy Gospel command
us to continue a perpetual memory of that
his precious death, until his coming again ...[4]

As Archbishop of Canterbury, Thomas Cranmer had influenced the souls of many, so it was essential that he be forced to return to the Catholic Church. His words were now considered heretical and dangerous. Was Christ's death and the church's celebration of it sufficient, or were there additional obligations for one to be certain of salvation? Could Christ's death alone forgive our sins? Was his death once for all (one oblation) or was he crucified again and again in the saying of the mass? These questions and more were answered in this one prayer. These were the issues that made martyrs of men and women.

Soon after Mary's coronation, Cranmer was arrested. It was a foregone conclusion that he was a heretic. For three years he was held prisoner. During this time he was moved from London to Oxford to make it more convenient for the theologians to debate him. Once his heresy was made official, they argued, begged, cajoled, and reasoned to get him to recant and give up his Protestant beliefs. In that day, if one recanted, it was understood that execution would be stayed and freedom returned. What Cranmer didn't know at the time was they were going to put him to death anyway.

By this time, Cranmer was already an old man of sixty-seven (the life of the average male was much less). He had accomplished many great things. And some not so great. Who knows what he regretted? Or exactly when he became a genuine believer? Or when he understood the full impact the Reformation would have on his theology and everyday life? Whatever the answers, at the end of his life, all he wished was to work in his garden, live in peace, and complete a book he was writing.

This desire must have tempted him to recant. Death, especially a painful death by fire, troubled him. If only he could die quietly, an old man, in his own bed. Perhaps it was to prey on these doubts that his jailers moved him several times between the miserable prison and his comfortable home nearby, in order to keep him troubled and uncertain. At last he signed the papers recanting his

Protestant faith, specifically standing against the "heresy of Luther and Zwingli." Rejoicing over their success, the authorities moved him back to prison and prepared to execute him.

On his last day, Cranmer was to appear in public to hear the sermon which was customarily preached before burning a heretic. Then he was to confirm aloud his return to the Catholic Church. At this point the recanting heretic normally was set free. Cranmer, however, must have realized during his final twenty-four hours that he wasn't to be spared after all.

Many turned out to hear the final proceedings and witness the spectacle: there were the theologians and bishops, members of the Queen's Council, noblemen, town officials, and commoners. Many were moved as they saw the grief on Cranmer's face and the tears that fell as he listened to the scathing sermon against him.

I wonder how often during that hour he recalled his own written prayers: "We have offended Almighty God . . . we have done that which we ought not to have done . . . there is no health in us . . . we are ashamed and sorry."

When at last they were done berating him, they turned in triumph to hear Cranmer's final confession. He pulled from his sleeve a prayer he had written, and began to pray. As he prayed, he wept:

> Oh, Father of Heaven.
> Oh, Son of God, Redeemer of the World.
> Oh, Holy Ghost, proceeding from Them both
> and Master of the World.
> Have mercy upon me most wretched caitiff[5]
> and miserable sinner;
> I, who have offended more grievously than any can
> express.
> Whither should I flee for succor?
> To Heaven I may be unable to lift up mine eyes;
> and in earth I find no refuge . . .
> Oh, Lord God, my sins be great,
> yet have mercy upon me for Thy great mercy.
> Oh God the Son,
> Thou was not made Man for few nor small offenses . . . .
> Although my sins be great, yet Thy Mercy is greater.
> I crave nothing, oh, Lord, for mine own merits,
> but for Thy Name's sake,
> that it may be glorified thereby,
> and for Thy Dear Son Jesus Christ's sake.[6]

Then to the amazement and horror of his accusers, he boldly proclaimed that in signing a recantation of his former beliefs, "my hand has offended in writing contrary to my heart. Therefore, my hand shall be first punished, for if I may come to the fire it shall be first burned."[7]

As the priests shouted to stop the mouth of the heretic, Cranmer ran from the church to the stake. Those who watched say that as he had vowed, he reached his right hand into the flames first. As the fire engulfed him he did not flinch from it, but was heard to say as long as he could: "This hand hath offended" and "Lord Jesus, receive my spirit."[8]

In Cranmer we see a great man, but one who was broken and humbled by his need of the cross even at the very end of his life. I usually picture martyrs as people who never hesitate, who from the first challenge cry out, "Kill me. I will never recant." If I were called upon to die like Cranmer, I would look for a way out, I would trail doubt in my wake as I stumbled and hesitated toward death, if I made it at all!

In Cranmer we witness the mysterious power of Christian faith: that through our weakness the power of God is revealed and his glory shines on us in the face of Christ (2 Cor. 4:6). This is one of the things I find so compelling about Christianity.

Surely, Cranmer stumbled on his journey to the stake, but he ran the final lap with the strength of Christ. One day I hope to meet him.

COOL COTTON SHEETS

SUMMER 1997

I stood in front of the freezer for five minutes with the door open until billows of fog began rolling out. I had forgotten what I was doing and had to shut the door, go back to the kitchen, and reorient myself. Reminding myself I needed to thaw something for supper, I went to the basement a second time. On the way, I grabbed some dirty laundry to drop off, and depositing that, forgot the freezer altogether. I went upstairs and stood at the sink, vaguely thinking, *Wasn't I going to do something else down there?*

It isn't only women who do this; men do the same thing. This is why you see them standing in the garage staring at the back wall for hours. They can't remember why they opened the door and walked in. Finally, they give up and begin to reshelve the tools left on the floor by the kids.

Forgetting where you are or what you're doing can be a sign of depression. The other day I went to our bedroom to water the plants and watered the trash basket instead. The next day, I took a package to UPS, paid for it, and left with it under my arm. The clerk called after me; "Hey, it's okay if you really *want* to deliver that yourself, but I could probably get it there a lot faster." During times like this, deciding what to wear can require as much effort as reading a software manual.

It's comforting to note that great men have often experienced the darkness of depression and despair. Samuel Rutherford, the Puritan preacher, once wrote to a friend: "I am at a low ebb as to any sensible communion with Christ; yea, as low as any soul can be, and do scarce know where I am."[1] In 1527 Martin Luther had nearly a year of sickness and intense depression. He was normally a prolific writer, publishing faster than most people could read. During that time his pen was silent. But out of that time came his most famous hymn, "A Mighty Fortress." He was able to find a measure of comfort in God, as one beautiful phrase reveals: "Our helper he amid the flood of mortal ills prevailing."

As an antidote to anxiety and to find comfort during suffering, Paul urges us to think about these things—things that are right. Pure. Admirable. Lovely (Phil. 4:8). These "things" Paul speaks of are often found all around us—as ordinary and unremarkable as the English sparrow or a dandelion.

Cool cotton sheets are an ordinary joy.

Jane Greer, a poet friend, notes that during a time of darkness, she could see nothing good about living. In desperation she asked God to show her one thing that could make her want more of life. That noon he gave her a "thing" to think about. As she ran errands, she passed two men jogging along the street. They were older, paunchy guys with big jelly-bellies wearing nothing but Speedos and running shoes. Their little twig arms and legs were very tan, so she knew they did this often. They paused at an intersection while the light changed and did that little jig runners do so their legs don't lock up. As they bounced there, in their tight Speedos with their bellies and breasts jiggling up and down, she suddenly knew that life was worth living.

She adds, "Understand that if I were to jog (which I would *never* do) nearly naked, these old guys would feel the same about me. God loves them and they were full of joy, as full as the most purely joyous thing I can think of, which is when my dog scratches her own back in her favorite two square feet of sweet clover with her tennis ball in her mouth, grinning."

There was a time when the psalmist wrote:

> My heart is not proud, O Lord . . . I do not concern myself with great matters or things too wonderful for me. But I have stilled and quieted my soul; like a weaned child with its mother, like a weaned child is my soul within me (Ps. 131:1–2).

When I am struggling to get through some anxious and ill times, I find it's the pleasure and hope of small matters that sustain me. The everyday. The ordinary. A purple finch who sings his heart out. A perfect, butter-yellow zinnia. Pure white cotton sheets dried in the sun and wind. Somehow these homey, simple things become markers in small, unexceptional packages that point to a Savior who is "altogether lovely." They remind me that a God who ministers to the tiniest bird can be trusted to care for the matters of my life and heart.

The summer has been difficult for our family, but suffering invites us to examine foundational beliefs to see whether they are sustainable during hard times. That is a good thing. We are comforted by and find hope in the humanity of Jesus as he is found in the Scriptures. He grew weary and thirsty, he wept with his friends when Lazarus died. Yet nothing fell through the cracks; no ship was wrecked because he couldn't make it to the disciples on time; no one missed getting healed because they had sinned too greatly or were too short to see him in the crowd.

This summer I often looked at the book of Hebrews, and especially the richness of chapter 12. We are told that you have not come to "darkness, gloom and storm; but to . . . Mount Zion, to the heavenly Jerusalem, the city of the living God. You have come to thousands upon thousands of angels in joyful company . . ." (vv 18–24). I'm not sure why the image of myriads of angels singing, or doing whatever it is they do, was so powerful to me during this time. Perhaps it was the reassurance that we have been invited, too. That the brokenness and depression we suffer will not be a game-changer or a reason for us to be left outside. All this made me weep. Today, we do not feel this joy the angels have, but we hope for it. The belief that God is able to keep us, body and soul, is enough to sustain me for now.

DO NOT OPEN UNDER PRESSURE

SUMMER 2000

Recently, my husband was making an espresso on our machine. He actually wanted the neighborhood coffee shop to make him one, but they refused because it was ten minutes until closing. In retrospect, perhaps he should have skipped it altogether. I could hear him in the kitchen moving around, opening cabinet doors and grinding beans.

As you probably know, a lot of steam is intentionally built up in the chamber of an espresso machine and we are expressly warned about this. In fact, this is written in English right on the equipment: *CAUTION: Do not remove coffee filter when under pressure!* From the living room I listened to the lovely shhhhisssss followed by the intense smell of French roast wafting through the air when suddenly I heard a loud POUFF!! as if someone shot a .22 rifle into a pillow. It was followed by a faint sprinkling sound. I knew right away what happened and yelled, "ARE YOU OKAY?" I received a mournful, "Yeeesss . . ."

Opening the chamber before the steam has cooled causes an explosion that blows finely ground coffee all over the kitchen and onto anyone standing nearby. We know that now. When I arrived at the scene, Denis was on his hands and knees wiping the floor. I did not add to his misfortune by silently pointing at the warning, I just grabbed a dishcloth and began quietly wiping off the counters while keeping my face averted. I know it's not nice to enjoy another's misery. But there was something amusing about my smart husband doing something, well, stupid.

A few days later we had another unfortunate explosion as we returned from an outing with our granddaughter in the late afternoon. Pulling the car into our garage on a bright afternoon is an act of faith. You assume everything is as you left it because the blinding light prevents you from seeing anything inside. So you aim for the darkened pit and slowly pull into the stall.

An unfortunate explosion.

We could not see that our house painter had left a gallon of unopened white paint in the tire track. When the car hit it, there was a loud explosion, and in the micro-second that followed, Denis thought we'd blown a tire, but in the next instant white paint blasted over the front of the car and the windshield. There was paint everywhere: dripping off the tools, the tarps, the lawnmower, and the bookcase I was refinishing. The garage looked like a gigantic Jackson Pollock painting. For thirty minutes, everyone worked like maniacs trying to remove the paint before it hardened.

The car is fine, but the paint permanently splashed on the garage floor will always remind us of the summer Toad Hall got painted, and we ran over a can of paint. I felt badly for our house painter, who was extremely apologetic, but especially for Denis. He was already weary to the bone because of other difficulties, and even though a look of infinite tiredness came over his face, he didn't utter one impatient word to our painter. I admired him for not even mildly cussing. The next day, he even laughed about it.

The troubles humans face are not only the life-shattering kind. Nearly everyone gets some of those. Life also gives us plenty of common, everyday trials that lead to body-and-soul weariness. In the midst of cleaning up the coffee grounds and the paint, we are supposed to keep going, loving and caring for others, but eventually, the stresses of life can begin to weigh too much. When I reach the margins of my coping ability, I start thinking crazy: *I'm never answering the phone again. If you complain about what I've made for supper, I quit. Do not ask to visit us because I don't plan to change the sheets on the guest bed until they rot.* Even minor mishaps can make a cursing mommy out of me.

Reaching this point seems to happen every summer about the time people really need a holiday. Suddenly, I want to leave everything and run away to what J.R.R. Tolkien calls *The Last Homely House, its doors flung wide.* The Last Homely House was a place of rest and refuge that existed on the edge of the dark and evil Misty Mountains through which the Hobbits had to travel. Of course, the weariness of their journey and the terrifying troubles the travelers faced made the place seem like heaven. Tolkien writes, "Bilbo would gladly have stopped there for ever and ever." Elrond's "house was perfect, whether you liked food, or sleep, or work, or story-telling, or singing, or just sitting and thinking best, or a pleasant mixture of them all." During their stay "their clothes were mended as well as their bruises, their tempers and their hopes."[1]

The Gospel of Mark tells us that on a day when Jesus' disciples were worn out from life (the context is instructive), "so many people were coming and going that they did not even have a chance to eat, he said to them, "Come with me by yourselves to a quiet place and get some rest" (Mark 6:31). What a beautiful invitation from the ultimate authority on weariness and the need for rest!

We recently spent a week at a lake cabin, where I could imagine settling down and staying for a long time, perhaps forever. It had all the things Tolkien mentions (except for the mending clothes part), including no visible neighbors, no telephone, and no email. We slept deeply without the sound of medical helicopters, sirens, and buses passing our house. The planets and stars swung silently through the night as the peepers trilled and the loons called. We ate grilled chicken and fresh berries. We drank wine in the evening and read P.D. James mysteries. I sat on the dock early one morning and watched a loon preen herself just a few feet away on the water. She rolled lazily onto her back, waggled a webbed foot in the air, and probed the white feathers of her breast. How peaceful and satisfying to do nothing more than look at God's creation. For the moment, there was a quiet joy for not having any trouble of my own, and of not knowing about yours.

However much we want to stay at the cabin, God won't allow it. Eventually we must leave again for the Misty Mountains. Throughout Scripture, God calls his people into his presence to bless and equip them for their work and calling. Then God essentially tells them: *You must go. You can't stay here. Not yet.* We can imagine David as a teenager, happily (we romantically assume) out in the fields caring for his sheep, killing lions, writing poetry, and composing music. Then one day, out of the blue, lightning strikes this bucolic scene. The prophet Samuel calls him in and anoints him to be king over Israel. David is going to be the best king Israel ever has. His descendants will sit on the throne forever; in fact, one of them will be Jesus Christ, The Son of David, and through him all people will be blessed.

This all sounds wonderful, but think of how many treacherous mountains David had to climb after that anointing. His troubles with Saul. Wars. The death of his closest friend, Jonathan. And becoming a fugitive, feigning mental illness to save his life, political intrigue, betrayal, adultery, murder, rape, family dysfunction, and attacks on his throne by his own son. The list goes on and on.

David's honesty about life is powerful. He prays to God: "Though you have made me see troubles, many and bitter, you will restore my life again; from the depths of the earth you will again bring me up" (Ps. 71:20).

For David to say, "You will restore my life again," implies that the things he has seen and endured (including his own sin) have taken a severe toll on his life, yet he believes God is able to restore life again. Psalm after psalm poured out of David's heart, leaving us a trail of life-saving caches to help us through the Misty Mountains. He models for us the trust in God that we desire, but that often escapes us. He demonstrates that, of all things, God is faithful, and he will bring us not only through this life, but to life eternal.

Meanwhile, after we rest awhile, God sends us back to daily life with all of its messiness. Tolkien, in writing his great trilogy, knows how difficult it is to leave Elrond's home. How difficult to be a pilgrim. As human beings, we long for the safety and beauty of Home. It's in our bones—that memory of the first Garden. Strider, the hobbits' guide and protector, gently corrects our impulse to stay in the cabin forever when he says of this place: "There my heart is; but it is not my fate to sit in peace, even in the fair house of Elrond."[2] But one day—one day when the Kingdom is fully restored—we will be allowed to stay.

It may seem pathetic that when I return to ordinary life, I must repeat, week after week, a home-keeping duty I detest: grocery shopping. I dislike it for a lot of reasons. It's never-ending because we always need to eat. Every week, I watch the food disappear in seconds, go back and do the same thing over again and again. I run to the store, bring home bags of food, only to return immediately because I've forgotten the toilet paper, which was very plainly written on the list, and which one cannot do without because all the Puffs are gone and we've started in on the paper towels.

Another reason I dislike shopping is that certain kinds of supermarket trickery make me angry. Recently, Hy-Vee had a type of plum which I happen to know are the best even though they are extremely ugly. They are called dinosaur eggs. The price was affordable, so I bought six. There were also some unusual peaches—little squashed round things called doughnut peaches. Again, ugly, but tasty. They were cheaper than *regular* peaches so I got a bag of them. As I was checking out and watching the totals, the plums rang up at $8.34 and the peaches were $6.80; this was *way* over my budget. At first, I was too stunned to protest. Then my eyes narrowed, and I got the feeling I was being suckered.

When the checker was done, I went back to the fruit to look and sure enough the plums were *not* $1.39 a pound. They were $1.39 *each*! The *each* was in very small, abbreviated print. Same thing with the peaches: they were $.68 *apiece*! I felt humiliated and swindled, so I just went home.

That evening I caught Denis eating one of the plums, and I shouted, "*What* are you *doing?* That plum cost $1.39!"

He looked at it thoughtfully and said: "Should I wait until it's rotten before I eat it?"

Later he tried to assuage my guilt for spending so much money on fruit by assuring me it was so good, he was quite sure they tasted more like $5.00 each, so actually it was a good deal.

I've always assumed that the older I get, the better I'll become at most things. I thought I would balance out the need to be engaged with life and the need to find restoration and rest without capsizing first. But apparently not. I find myself obsessing over my failure to read grocery store signs more carefully, and then not having the courage to return the merchandise and get my money back. Translate that feeling into bigger, more important things like relationships and responsibilities to people and work. I feel more need for wisdom and more practice in the fundamentals of love, patience, and forgiveness than ever. Which is why all of the above, from Jesus' invitation to *come away* to David's confession about his troubles being *many and bitter* continually give me hope that with God's help, I will endure to the end.

Saint Francis de Sale's instructions apply so particularly to people like myself:

> Go on in all simplicity, do not be so anxious to win a quiet mind, and it will be all the quieter. Do not examine so closely into the progress of your soul. Do not crave so much to be perfect, but let your spiritual life be formed by your duties, and by the actions which are called forth by circumstances. Do not take overmuch thought for tomorrow. God, who has led you safely on so far, will lead you on to the end. Be altogether at rest in the loving holy confidence which you ought to have in His heavenly Providence.[3]

CALL THE FBI

SUMMER 2002

A few years ago, our neighbor, Susan, rang the doorbell. That wasn't so remarkable, but since it was the third time that day... She was looking rather worse. Her hair was disheveled, her eyes had dark circles under them, she smelled strongly of cigarettes and mildew, and she was shaking.

"Can I use your phone?" She sounded frightened.

I invited her inside.

"I need to call the FBI in Minneapolis," she explained on her way to the kitchen where our phone was mounted on the wall.

I knew she'd been having trouble with the neighbor on the other side of her house, and assumed he may have finally done something really criminal. Ted was an aggressive, angry man who harassed all his neighbors. One time he chased our son down the street, across our yard, and onto our porch because Jerem rode his bike on newly-laid asphalt in the alley. Ted had almost caught up to him when Jerem slammed through the front door screaming, "DAAAAD!" The terror in his voice brought us both running. That was the kind of neighbor he was.

He particularly bullied Susan about how she kept her yard. Once, out of pure malice, he aimed his paint sprayer over the fence at the freshly painted siding on her house. His paint was white. Hers was a dark pine green. When Susan found it, he loftily claimed it was wind drift, and he couldn't help *that.* Susan wept because the whole backside of her house was ruined.

It's true Susan was a hoarder and her yard was a bit of an eyesore because she collected things other people threw away. Raccoons, squirrels, and mice (and someone was sure they'd seen rats) all lived in her small yard. On the other hand, the rock wall she built along the front sidewalk and the wild cottage garden look of her flowers had a fascinating mix of chaos and beauty.

But this time, it wasn't Ted who was bothering her. She explained someone had broken into her house and stolen all her important papers: the deed to her house, her insurance papers, the car title, bank receipts. She had searched and searched. They were nowhere to be found; she knew it had to have been a burglar. She begged us to keep an eye on her home and report any suspicious activity, and we promised to do it.

She had finally gone to the police station to report this theft, and they sent an officer to inspect the premises. He reported no sign of forced entry, and since there was unbroken snow in the yard surrounding the house, he could tell no one had walked up and climbed in through a window. She was not reassured by this, so she went back to the station to pressure them a little more, and while she was waiting, she told me, the oddest thing happened. She left her purse on the chair for just a moment to get a drink from the fountain in the hall. When she returned she saw that someone had been rifling through her purse and had stuffed every single missing paper back inside!

That was when she began to piece together what was going on. She knew her little house and property were very valuable, being a corner lot and prime real estate. The local newspaper had reported that the Mayo Clinic was desperate for more parking space for its employees. Susan's house was only two blocks from St. Mary's, the clinic's largest hospital, so wasn't it obvious that the police and Mayo were involved in a conspiracy to steal her property, tear down her house, and build a parking lot? However, she reported that when she was down at the station the second time, the police could see that she was not to be trifled with. They began having second thoughts about harassing her and had found the perfect opportunity to return all her papers, and then accuse *her* of being crazy.

The thought that she could not trust the police was so frightening, and she so desperately needed to feel safe that she was trying to reach the FBI in Minneapolis for help and protection. When she called, all she ever got was an answering machine: *Please leave your name, phone number, and a brief summary of your problem, and we will get back to you.* Over the next several days, she used our phone to call them four or five more times, leaving desperate messages and begging for help. She asked us to please continue watching her house, and if we saw any strangers trying to get in, to please help her. I assured her we absolutely would. Then she and I looked at each other helplessly because who do you call when you suspect a crime and the police are complicit?

She was so convincing, one could almost believe her. But we knew something about Susan (who has since passed away): she had a mental illness. Psychiatrists had labeled her a paranoid schizophrenic. But in getting to know her, we learned she was far more than her medical diagnosis.

Clearing out the home of our neighbor, Susan.

True, she was eccentric, and sometimes confused, but mental illness did not reflect all of who she was. We saw evidence of this again and again. She was resourceful and creative; I loved how she hauled bricks from a demolition site blocks away on an old lawnmower bed. She had replaced the engine with boards to make a platform. Trip after trip and hundreds of pounds made a huge pile in her driveway. From those bricks she laid a beautiful patio and a walk through her flowers. When her roof needed to be replaced, she did it herself. Painstakingly, bit by bit. Up and down the ladder, day after day, carrying a few shingles at a time. And all her neighbors shared in the disposal of her old roof, because late at night as we slept she put the shingles in grocery sacks and deposited them in our trash cans.

She taught me how to mix mortar and build a little garden wall with stones. She gave me a recipe for pickled crab apples. She played Jelly Roll Morton on our piano. We talked about Russian authors and argued about whether Dostoyevsky was better than Tolstoy. Many times I saw her sitting on her stone steps, half-hidden behind tall oxeye daisies and her rotting '65 Mustang ("A collector's car, you know. I've been offered thousands for it"), sorting through bags of old clothes or reading the newspaper, and I would bring her a plate of our supper to share. Her keen pleasure in the food kept me doing it again and again. To my everlasting benefit, she proved to me that even though she had a serious mental health problem, she was a beautiful human being, a good friend, and God-endowed with unique gifts.

I thought more about her after watching *A Beautiful Mind*, the movie based on the life of mathematician John Nash, because it caused me to reflect more on what it must be like to suffer with a mental illness. One of the things that struck me is how the film director almost forces the viewer to identify with the terrifying and confusing mental storms Nash endured. I remember when the camera led us out to his study, a little shack in the back yard, where we assumed Nash had been spending fruitful hours working on his research. As the door opened and we looked in, we were hopeful we might see evidence of his recovery. Instead we saw hundreds and hundreds of bits of paper painstakingly pinned to the walls until every square inch was covered with urgent messages and codes. We knew immediately that we were seeing the terrible state of his mind. My eyes welled with tears of dread because I had grown to care about him. I saw he was more than just his illness, more than a mathematical genius: He was a man of wit and humor, a human being, who despite his suffering, had extraordinary gifts in mathematics. To our wonder and delight, in real life, John Nash eventually won the Nobel Prize for economic sciences.

I have friends who suffer from mental illnesses in varying intensities. This movie reminded me of how much they must endure in order to live, work, and relate to people, and of what courage it must take to keep on with daily life. Just as having any type of chronic illness does not rule out the contributions one can make to the body of Christ, so also the one who suffers from depression, bipolar, schizophrenia, or eating disorders still has much to give that enriches our lives the same as anyone. As Christians, we too often contribute to their loneliness and humiliation by making it unsafe for them to admit they have a mental illness.

I have a friend who leans hard against recurring depression; she told me that one Sunday she walked into our church and noticed a brochure on how Christians can defeat depression. Curious, she picked it up and learned the author believed that basically if you want to get well, then you ought to begin by confessing your sin and bringing your life under the Lordship of Christ. Then get yourself up, dust off your hands, and get on with life. Despite the risk of having to admit she struggled with depression, she talked to the pastor after the service and told him it is rarely that simple. She told that there were many reasons and situations, other than unconfessed sin, that might cause depression. One of them might be a chemical imbalance that no amount of pulling yourself together is going to fix, and that she herself was on a medication for depression and found it very discouraging to find such literature contributing to misinformation. The pastor looked at her and said nothing. He gave no response, he just moved on. That was many months ago, and the brochure still sits on the back table. Sadly, what this means for our Christian friends with mental illnesses is that they continue to hide in our midst, pretending to be okay in public while privately suffering alone.

David Hilfiker, MD, writes that his lifelong experience with depression is manifested by a singular lack of joy; and yet he participates in the life of the church in prayer, worship, daily Bible reading, and in corporate missions. He works as a physician to homeless men with AIDS. Some Christians insist that one of the marks of true spirituality is the joy you feel in your life. Following Christ has not done this for him. Yet he would attest that God is faithful and it has been his Christian community who holds him dear, and who represent God's love for him that keeps him going. He likens his mental illness to a spiritual paradox.

Hilfiker believes that if we can accompany one another through the messy reality of life, it can bring wisdom and a measure of healing. We discover that our journeys together, with all their messiness, bring us closer to our deepest selves and to our littleness, and indeed, bring us closer to God. This, he claims, is a paradox of the highest order, understood by only the deepest spiritualities: it is precisely through our brokenness that we touch God.[1] I would add, it is also through our brokenness that God touches us.

What I have discovered in these particular examples is more confirmation, as if it were needed, that all are made in the image of God, and as such we have meaning and purpose beyond any objective material witness. There is a peculiar humanness which allows us to grasp at the transcendent and appreciate the beauty of creation. In turn we are able to create something even out of suffering and give it as a gift to another—sometimes unwittingly.

The ability of the mentally ill to give gifts to others, despite their suffering, is not only observed by perceptive Christians. I was deeply moved by author Oliver Sacks, who wrote *The Man Who Mistook His Wife for a Hat*. Sacks has professed no particular faith that I am aware of, and yet he helps us see that even profoundly impaired people again and again prove to be more than just a medical case unable to transcend their disease. In the midst of suffering they reveal a human soul, a hunger for the spiritual, a god-likeness for which there is no satisfactory scientific explanation.

As a clinical neurologist, Dr. Sacks recounts with compassion and insight the lives of people who have suffered incredible adversity—patients whose lives seem to have no meaning beyond suffering from neurological illness. He tells about a man whose experience of amnesia was so profound, he had no "day before." Jimmy's face expressed infinite sadness and loss, but when asked how he felt, could not tell whether he *felt badly or not*. He had lost all ability to organize or remember the present. He could not remember isolated items more than a few minutes.

One day Sacks asked the sisters at the Catholic Home where Jimmy lived whether they thought he had a soul. They were outraged by the question and said he should watch Jimmy in chapel and then judge for himself. He wrote:

> I was profoundly moved and impressed because I saw here an intensity and steadiness of attention and concentration that I had never seen before in him or conceived him capable of. I watched him kneel and take the Sacrament on his tongue, and could not doubt the fullness and totality of communion, the perfect alignment of his spirit with the spirit of the Mass. Fully, intensely, quietly, in the quietude of absolute concentration and attention, he entered and partook of the Holy communion. He was no longer at the mercy of… meaningless sequences and memory traces—but was absorbed in an act, an act of his whole being, which carried feeling and meaning in an organic continuity and unity, a continuity and unity so seamless it could not permit any break.
>
> And always for a while after communion his mood of quietness and peace would persist in a way not seen in the rest of his life at the Home.[2]

In the Church, we often avoid those who suffer from mental illnesses—the very ones who often already suffer as outcasts from family, friends, and community. They are even cast aside by their own souls; yet our privilege is to call them beloved of Christ and integral to our body. It isn't only that they need us—we need them if we are to believe Scripture. Paul writes, "Those parts of the body which seem weaker are indispensable" (1 Cor .12:22).

I confess I have discovered a contemptible prejudice against mental illness in myself. It came as a revelation at the doctor's office when I was referred to a psychiatrist to renew a sleep medication often prescribed for people who have fibromyalgia. (One of the symptoms is sleep disorder.) At first I thought, *No problem. Whatever it takes.* Then I went home and began to fuss. A psychiatrist! What did my primary care doctor really have in mind? She was looking at me funny. On the surface it was a meds consult, but was that her true agenda or does she think I'm crazy?

My appointment made me really nervous. I sat in the doctor's office trying to sit still. I told myself to stop swallowing my spit and keep my hands off my face, but I couldn't. The psychiatrist was a young man, almost too young to be my son. I wondered what he was doing there, he looked like a model from Abercrombie

& Fitch. He kept his handsome face carefully neutral as he leaned forward a bit and spoke from behind his big desk: "I'll be taking notes as we talk and I don't want you to worry about that." Well. Until you mentioned it. He paused to stare intently at me until I wondered if there was something stuck in my teeth. Then he asked, "So. Why do you think you're here today?" Feeling insulted and irrational, I nearly said, "Because I started my husband's bed on fire?" Regaining control in the nick of time, I carefully reported: "My doctor said it was to consult with you about this medication and also to see whether you think I should be referred to biofeedback for muscle relaxation therapy. If she had other reasons she didn't mention them." (Maybe just a tiny bit hostile.)

My mind was racing ahead, wondering how many invasive questions he would ask and whether it was safe to be honest. Does he think I'm a crazy fifty-something woman with a hysterical, hypochondriacal personality? Oh. Isn't that a symptom of paranoia? But what if I am? Wouldn't it be safe to face it there? Should I be ashamed to get help if I need it?

He did ask me about depression and other moods. I decided to be honest and admitted, "Anxiety is my chiefest, most nuts, mental flaw." I plunged on: "Or character defect. Whatever you'd like to call it. I work hard at not being anxious and this here is making me damn nervous."

He nodded and scribbled away. Now to his credit and none to mine, he was kind, insightful, and he also cleverly sniffed out my evasions. After about twenty minutes I had stopped sweating and gulping air. By the end of the hour he okayed the meds and told me with a grin that I didn't need to see him again. I still left feeling like I'd been rescued from Desolation Island in the Antarctic Ocean. Just to breathe air in the parking lot was exhilarating.

The more I reflected on my reaction to this encounter, the more I realized how revealing my attitude was. It's just fine for you to have any number of mental illnesses. As our four-year-old granddaughter says, "I am your fren." From bipolar to simple depression, I'm okay with *you* having it. It doesn't make *you* less of a person. Blah, blah, blah. And then I had that little trick played on me, and found out it isn't okay for *me*. Suddenly I have to confess how sorry I am to be this kind of bigot.

And now that I think of it, the courage of some of my friends who have had to be hospitalized, therapied, medicated, shocked, and sent to group with clueless "facilitators" and know-nothing "peers" is surpassing wonderful bravery. And I thank them for understanding my fear better than anyone and for continuing to be my friend despite my prejudices. In turn, I promise that I will never say again, when expressing relief about some medical diagnosis, "I'm so glad it wasn't in my head!"

Finally, one last plug. There is a book . . . are you surprised? *Resurrecting the Person: Friendship and the Care of People with Mental Health Problems,* by John Swinton. Called a book of practical theology, Swinton issues a challenge to the church to think and act differently toward people and families whose lives have been radically altered by mental health problems. He explores ways of separating people from their pathologies both practically and conceptually. He suggests Jesus as a model for countercultural friendship with those who have been marginalized and alienated by society.

Although I do not agree entirely with his theology, I can't find anything on the market so personally helpful and hopeful when it comes to exploring deep and meaningful friendship with a person who struggles with a mental health problem. I strongly recommend this book for anyone. We should be starving for this kind of help. We need it for the sake of Jesus. For the sake of his bride, the church. Who knows when you yourself may suffer from an unwanted mental illness?

EATING THE EASTER BUNNY

SPRING 2004

You know, there's a reason why they call those free range, organic chicken breasts in the supermarket "Smart Brand." As opposed to raising and butchering them yourself? You have no idea how much smarter it is. We tried it for a while, my husband and me. That was back when our thinking was crystalline, and we tried to convince everyone to become urban farmers and save the earth. In our backyard we were going to raise earthworms. I forget exactly why, but I think the worms were supposed to transform our hard New Mexican soil into loam and the sale of leftover boxes full of writhing worms were going to fund our retirement or something. We actually did grow a big garden, raise bees, and breed rabbits—the French equivalent to chickens.

I can't even begin to remember how I got my husband to agree to do this last thing. He is no carpenter, but somehow he managed to build three sturdy rabbit cages. I believe a friend helped him—it was a long time ago.

Through the want ads we bought a big white New Zealand buck and two does. One of the does was also a New Zealand white who cast huge litters of brilliant white bunnies. Our son, Jerem, must have been two years old when he set them all free in our backyard one afternoon. It looked like it had snowed in a Looney Tunes, as bunnies ran in drifts, joyfully leaping one another and kicking off the back wall.

The second doe was an unknown breed the color of burnished chestnut who produced dozens of babies with color combinations only God could think of. Pairing the white male with her hidden genes made bunnies of pure black, black and white, brown and white, or Siamese with a fawn body and delicate black points. We fell in love, forgetting that the end of this short food chain meant we were supposed to kill and eat them.

I do recall every detail of what it took to dispatch and cook them, including our daughter's suspicious question at the dinner table: *What is this?* And my quick lie: *Fried chicken, it's just fried chicken, so eat it.* I won't recount our personal butchering details for you right now, but I did recently come across this description in a book which is so proximate to what we experienced, I can hear the sounds and smell the blood.

> The purveyor appeared with twelve live rabbits. "He knocked one out, slit its throat, pinned it to a board, skinned it, gutted it, the whole bit," Keller[1] remembers. "Then he left." Alone in the grass behind the restaurant with eleven little bunnies, he lurched for the first victim. "Rabbits scream," Keller says. "And this one screamed really loud." Keller tried to kill it, but the rabbit struggled to get away. The rabbit nearly broke free, but Keller gripped it by the leg, and the leg snapped in his hand. Terrified and now likely in great pain, the rabbit could no longer run, and Keller managed to kill it.
>
> Thus did Keller learn how to butcher a rabbit, and it had been an unhappy experience . . . killing these rabbits had been so horrible for him, had so humbled him, he would not squander their lives. He determined to use all his powers as a cook to ensure that these were the best rabbits ever.
>
> —Michael Ruhlman[2]

Americans have moved far from the process of butchering. A lot of us have sworn off meat-eating because we are so convinced of the rightness for health or morality that we can't even bear to trap the mice living in the couch or the spider making a web behind the toilet. Most of us are so distant from the family farm and rural life, we've lost even secondhand experience of the cost of blood and butchering. If we buy meat at all, it's sealed in plastic and perched on a white tray with a diaper underneath to absorb offensive liquid. Some of us are lucky enough to get a tiny jolt of reality when the child we take to a petting zoo suddenly connects a silky feathered crowing rooster with that piece of lean, white meat thawing on the counter for supper.

Last fall our five-year-old granddaughter went with Grandpa to a farm where he picked out our Thanksgiving turkey. Making the connection to our annual feast, Manessah swore she would never eat turkey again. Ever.

It was troublesome. But when the day came, she was won over by the rich, golden smell and the juicy slices of breast meat on the platter.

Raising those rabbits and forcing ourselves to kill them had its special reward—which may be difficult to believe. I don't think it's meant to be easy, but I get what it means to take the life of a living creature and eat it so you can live. I'm also grateful that on a strange, historic day, God blessed the ritual of eating meat together by accepting an invitation from Abraham to stay for lunch.

> The LORD appeared to Abraham near the great trees of Mamre while he was sitting at the entrance to his tent in the heat of the day. Abraham looked up and saw three men standing nearby. When he saw them, he hurried from the entrance of his tent to meet them and bowed low to the ground…
>
> "Let a little water be brought, and then you may all wash your feet and rest under this tree. Let me get you something to eat, so you can be refreshed… then he ran to the herd and selected a choice, tender calf and gave it to a servant, who hurried to prepare it. He then brought some curds and milk and the calf that had been prepared and set these before them. While they ate, he stood near them under a tree. (Genesis 18:1–8).

The Scriptures teem with symbols and rituals meant to remind us of what it cost God to pay for what has gone wrong in the world. From the beginning in the garden, when God sent Adam and Eve on their way after giving them leather clothing and permission to eat meat, all the way to the courtyards of the Jerusalem temple where payment included the slaying of animals for sacrifice, blood has been shed. For generations, Israel slaughtered lambs, offered them, ate them, and looked for the Messiah to come and pay up the cost of sin for real, forever. The price of wrong-doing has been a bloody mess and we are at fault for it.

Jerem holds one of our New Zealand whites—an iconic Easter bunny.

Paul reminds us of the fatal breaking of Christ's body:

> And when He had given thanks, He broke it and said, "Take, eat; this is My body which is broken for you; do this in remembrance of Me." In the same manner He also took the cup after supper, saying, "This cup is the new covenant in My blood. This do, as often as you drink it, in remembrance of Me." For as often as you eat this bread and drink this cup, you proclaim the Lord's death till He comes. (1 Corinthians 11:24–26 NKJV)

Now, in the church we *celebrate* the Lord's supper. To celebrate is to observe an event with ceremonies of festivity and rejoicing. To reach the point of celebration over Jesus death, it is first necessary to understand his suffering and why he had to die. I think what Mel Gibson's movie *The Passion* does best for us is to help us understand the outrageous physical cost.

Before the huge media blitz over this movie, I grew tired of all the Christian hype, the interviews, the campaigns, and reviews. A young friend commented before it was released: "I'm already so sick of hearing about this movie and how we need to use it as an evangelistic tool, and how can we get our neighbors to this and corner them about what they've seen and what they're going to do about it. I don't even know if I want to see it. What about just going and viewing it as a film, a piece of art that is meant to touch our own lives in a deep and real way?"

He expressed my own vague discomfort over the endless Christian hoopla, even though my saying anything negative about using *The Passion* to bring lost sinners to Christ sounds heretical. Like I don't believe in the virgin birth or something.

In fact, I can understand non-Christians feeling suspicious of our motives if we suddenly become interested in knowing what *they* think about a movie. We've never asked before! Recently there have been plenty of movies which bring up the big questions of life (What's the meaning of life? Where did I come from? What happens after death? Etc.). But if I suddenly take an interest in what you as my non-Christian neighbor think of *this* one, just now because it perfectly fits my version of what Christ's life was about and can therefore drive our "discussion"? Isn't that a little disingenuous?

I value *The Passion* for its unblinking look at the physical suffering Jesus endured during the last hours of his life—the beating, the staggering to the place of execution, the drinking of life's poison, and the crashing of all his body's systems. That's what this movie does so well.

Although I really do want to reach my neighbor, the power of this movie may lie more in its ability to confront me with my tendency to make the cross just another bad day in the life of Jesus. Another day in which we have to butcher a gentle calf or the baby rabbits.

I may be in touch with what it costs an animal for me to live, but I can callously ignore what it cost Jesus to forgive me for the wrongs I've committed. I'm filled with an enormous capacity to excuse my "little" infractions—see above lie I told our daughter. And furthermore, every time UPS delivers another review copy of some new book, I'm filled with undisguised envy. *Yes,* I think. *Someone else has written another book? Bah!*

I'm also quick to note how others have wronged me. Tim Keller, pastor of Redeemer Presbyterian in Manhattan, says there is something wrong with our spiritual memory—we remember an insult or an unanswered prayer hundreds of times longer, while our ability to remember something good is, oh, maybe thirty seconds.

For example, although it has been more than a month since we received this message on our answering machine from JOEL in Minnesota, I remember every word: "I'm calling with a request to be continued on the mailing list for *Critique,*[3] but would not care to receive *Notes From Toad Hall.* So if you can continue to do the mailing for *Critique,* that's all I'm really interested in."

Oh, yeah?

Furthermore, my attitude toward Denis, whom I love more than anyone in all the world I can be . . . well, here, from my journal:

> Denis and I have had some marital snaps. I feel insulted by his pointed questions. I take it very personally when he peers at my computer screen and asks, "What have you done?!" *I'VE DONE NOTHING AT ALL. BILL GATES DID IT*, I say. Though Denis swears no personal intent, I am certain he does. And off we go, snap, snap, snap. We both feel misunderstood and angry. One moment we're so in love we can't believe our luck and the next we're ready to bite off the other's head.
>
> This depresses Denis. But I'm more callous. I shrug. This is merely life. I forgive you, you forgive me, and now let's cuddle like we always do. Okay?

This is why Jesus fell on the road to Calvary? *This* is why he had to cry "My God, my God, why have you forsaken me" (Matt. 27:46)? To pay for my stupid little sins? That is what's so hard to get my mind around. That he should care enough to drink my poison. And that's why Gibson's artistic depiction of Christ's suffering in those final hours reminds me to cast my entire lot in with Christ. How can we resist such love?

This love is what makes the Eucharist such a celebration. That, and knowing the ugly things we've done weren't able to keep Jesus dead at all. God raised him and, man, we should be dancing in the streets. If only we weren't white Norwegian Presbyterians!

I WANT WHAT THE CAT ATE

SPRING 2004

Our local newspaper reported that in a small town near Rochester, a man driving his van along a river saw a bald eagle swoop down and grab a sixteen-inch sucker from the water. Larry Knight slowed to watch. "I thought it was really awesome to watch an eagle fly into the creek and pick a fish up," he said.

The eagle struggled to gain altitude with the extra weight. You know, after an eagle grabs a fish, it quickly adjusts its hold so the fish slices through the air, decreasing the drag. (I learned this from David Attenborough's *Life of Birds* video series. It's very cool how they grasp it along the spine with one claw in front of the other.) It's apparently not so easy to "mount up on wings of an eagle" when you're trying to shift a slapping, slippery fish.

This eagle lost its grip as it ascended over the top of Larry's van. The dropped fish shattered his windshield and exploded guts and fish eggs over the front of the van. Larry says the van is now sitting in his driveway because the insurance company claims they don't cover damage from flying fish. He also reports that the neighbor's cat ate what was left on the vehicle. He decided the next time he sees an eagle carrying a fish he won't be stopping to watch. "I'm givin' her the gas," he said.

At first, I thought I might identify with the driver: you stop to admire God's creation, thinking that by it you will gain a deeper understanding of God, but as you draw near, his handiwork contrives to injure you. You are struck by the apparent random nature of misfortune and God's plan for your spiritual growth—like when, for the first time as an adult, you decide to give yourself completely to Christ and the next two years are the worst of your life.

Then I thought, perhaps the eagle serves as the main point in this story; he scores high for trying. It didn't work out this time, but he's not going to stop fishing. So I'm the eagle, I've caught the fish, and yes, I've dropped it, and made a big mess, but I'm not giving up. Remember "You will soar on wings like eagles" (Isa.

40:31). It's the verb that defines when that will be achieved. Notice "you will" is future tense. I'm not quite mounting up on wings today. Maybe I've lost the prize fish. Tomorrow, or, at the very least, in the next life, I will be more like Jesus, so I will keep on trying to fly, I will keep fishing, because one day I'm going to carry that darn fish back to my nest and eat it.

In the end, it isn't the driver *or* the eagle I fully appreciate in this allegory of life. It's the cat. Imagine him on the same old, same old stealth inspections of the neighborhood, making rounds to back doors, the flower pots, the roll-away trash bin. Just a routine, ordinary night out marking his territory. Suddenly he sniffs the surprising odor of fish eggs and guts wafting off the hood of a van. (Never mind how unlikely the spot—God often reveals himself on detours. Think about Moses turning aside to investigate the burning bush.) There, amidst shards of glass is the most unexpected and exquisite of pleasures—sucker roe. He leaps up, his pink tongue and needle teeth pulling away sacs and veins (it's a dangerous feast, but, oh, so worth it). It's Christ, beckoning us from among the broken flower pots and trash bins, *come dine with me.* I want to be the cat.

I would like to feast on something nourishing with Jesus, but I'm in a spiritual funk. As I trudge through my daily rounds, to the kitchen, to the store, to the office, I'm keeping an eye out for some word, some yummy fish eggs that will move me out of a spiritual desert. In my search, I come across a quote from Eugene Peterson. I have a feeling he knows me well.

> First, Christian spirituality, the contemplative life, is not about us. It is about God. The great weakness of American spirituality is that it is all about us: fulfilling our potential, getting the blessings of God, expanding our influence, finding our gifts, getting a handle on principles by which we can get an edge over the competition. The more there is of us, the less there is of God.
>
> Christian spirituality is not a life-project for becoming a better person. It is not about developing a so-called deeper life. We are in on it, to be sure, but we are not the subject. Nor are we the action. We get included by means of a few prepositions: God with us (Matt. 1:23), Christ in me (Gal. 2:20), God for us (Rom. 8:31). With, in, for: They are powerful, connecting, relation-forming words, but none of them makes us either the subject or the predicate. We are the tag-end of a prepositional phrase.
>
> Sooner or later in this life we get invited or commanded to do something. But in that doing, we never become the subject of the Christian life nor do we perform the action of the Christian life. We are invited or commanded into what I call prepositional

> participation. The prepositions that join us to God and God's action in us within the world—the *with,* the *in,* the *for*—are very important, but they are essentially a matter of the ways and means of being in on and participating in what God is doing.[1]

I want to participate in what God is doing, but how? His Word is life to me. I spend time in it because it does change me in subtle, mysterious ways. The people who know me best, my mother and my husband, claim to know when I neglect this spiritual discipline. But there are times when I despair of reading the Bible, times when nothing resonates, nothing strikes. Losing a sense of the reality of God's presence in my life increases my hunger for something solid.

When I'm experiencing spiritual dryness, my first instinct is to do exactly what Tim Keller describes in a sermon on Psalm 42. He says that when something goes wrong for American Christians, they look for someone or something to pin it on. We tend to be very moralistic and think that surely spiritual dryness is the result of unconfessed sin in our life. We haven't pushed the right button, we've neglected our Christian "to-do list."

What we need to grasp, he says, is that dryness is going to happen no matter where, who, or how old you are as a Christian. It isn't necessarily because you've done something wrong, or haven't had faith, or neglected to read through the Bible in a year. It's because you're human and live in a fractured, fallen world.

When discouraged, I look to the little things in life. When can Margie have a latte? When can she eat some chocolate? When can she sit in the sun, listen to music, read a good story, think of a clever status update? Making Self my integrative personal center can be disappointing, because these things can't sustain my soul for very long. The psalmist knows this and declares a shift: "Hope in God," he tells himself (Ps. 42:5). And he begins to think about *chesed*—the Hebrew word for God's loving-kindness. He recounts his personal history and all the times God helped him. Since he is also a professional musician and a poet, he turns the grace of God into a song he sings to himself through the night: "By day the Lord directs his love, at night his song is with me" (v. 8). Again, mysteriously, these words become a sweet grace at the just the right time.

I was still looking for "what the cat ate" last week as I was updating the calendar and thinking nothing more could fit into my schedule. That's when I got an early morning phone call. At first, all I heard were stifled sobs and sniffling. As soon as I determined it was our five-year-old granddaughter, I relaxed a little. It wasn't the dreaded call announcing someone you love has been killed in a car accident. It was Manessah and she wanted to talk.

She'd just awakened from a bad dream and couldn't shake it. She'd been to the zoo with her little friend, Gracey, and inexplicably found herself alone

Stealing away granddaughter on a summer day.

on a bus to Rochester, but she couldn't find our house. She felt like I was lost from her. You know that nightmarish feeling when you urgently need to reach someone and you can't? On the phone she said, "I need to see you because we are moving very far away and I won't see you anymore." It's true, they are moving to Tennessee.

At the time, I was in the process of writing an issue of *Notes From Toad Hall.* It was due at the printer and I hadn't even gotten it to my layout editor yet, so I was really late. We weigh these things, don't we? What's most important? What trumps this or that? Especially, how do we manage deadlines that pit them against the needs of those we love? Sometimes the person who really needs you can't tell you. I noticed this about our children, and I continue to see it in the children of our friends. Adult obligations, meetings, appointments appear so pressing and important, even older children know they can't say, couldn't you drop that meeting? Just stay home and do nothing? Hang out with me in case I think of something important like where's my allowance, or what would you think if I got a tattoo? That sort of being present with someone means: don't invite anyone else to join you, don't answer the phone, and especially, don't email or text while we're talking.

The next day I left the office behind with its unanswered letters and unfinished writing. Things could wait until the next day. And they did.

Sometimes when we set aside what appears to be costly time to be with someone, we think it will be historic. We imagine the slaking of our spiritual thirst will involve something epic like a voice from heaven. Some of us think it might include the sharing of unforgettable music, food, books, and conversation so deep life will never be the same. But this is how it actually was for my thirsty little soul.

I drove to Minneapolis and snuck Manessah out of school. The day was mild and sunny, and the waves on Lake Calhoun were very blue, as Manessah pointed out. I took her to a really cool children's bookstore, The Wild Rumpus, where they have cats curled up in easy chairs, and real live chickens wandering around. They do! The little white hen with feathers on her feet, who allows you to pet her, laid an egg on the floor under a bookshelf, and Manessah picked it up while it was still warm. We looked at books and bought *Ramona, the Pest* by Beverly Cleary. We stopped for an ice cream cone at an old fire station-turned-shop. Later, we ate lunch at McDonald's, capping it off with a McFlurry.

The conversation that drifted from the backseat of the car was not profound:

"I'm hungry, can we get a cheeseburger? I would love the puppy they give with Happy Meals."

"I wonder if people will think you're my mother?"

Me: "Probably not. I'm a bit older than your mother."

Quietly, to herself: "That's right. She has white hair, and she's very, very, very old."

Then, she sang the names of the continents to the tune of "Twinkle, Twinkle Little Star."

When I left, she hugged me tight and thanked me for "stoling" her away from school. I promised when they moved, I would write her, call her, and we would visit them in Tennessee. What she gave me was surely more than what I gave to her. We had a just-right, ordinary, every-day time.

So I'm back with the cat who discovered fish eggs on the van. There are no reliable predictors for where you'll find a yummy feast or what person will become your drink in the desert. Or which Scripture God may use to give you hope for the day.

THE ANNUAL AMERICAN CHRISTMAS LETTER

WINTER 2004

There's a basket on our dining room table which collects all the beautiful cards, letters, and photos we receive over the holidays. There are new jobs, new family members, new homes, and new fitness. There are reunions, graduations, promotions, and trips. I love to read these accounts and see the pictures as it's a way of keeping up with old friends. I always mean to answer each one personally, but by July, when the letters are still sitting there unanswered, I abandon the idea. It was a good idea, but I just couldn't do it.

Most of the letters are glowing accounts of all the incredible things accomplished by family members. Behind these shining words, only a few brave ones hint there might have been mistaken choices, loneliness, doubt, and times of difficulty or depression.

It makes me wonder about the message we send when we present an "Everything's GREAT" picture of life to our friends and family. We want to rejoice with friends over the good things that come to us, but what about the teens who slam the doors, the frozen pipe that burst on the second floor while we were in Hawaii, the job we lost, or the accident we were responsible for? How dishonest or damaging is our flawless life picture to a weary person or family struggling to survive in a broken world? Or are we the only ones who face trouble?

I've wondered what the stories of Scripture would sound like if I'd been the one in charge of editing and protecting God's perfect image. Or what if I were an Old Testament patriarch responsible for getting out the news about our family? I may have put a different spin on things. This year I experimented with that idea, and wrote two versions of an annual Christmas letter written by Jacob, son of Isaac.

JACOB'S ANNUAL CHRISTMAS LETTER, VERSION ONE

Dear ones back in Ur,

Since our family moved to Canaan, we haven't seen many of you and it's been way too long since I have written. You probably recall it was my Grandfather Abraham who first moved out this way. We've been very busy these past years, so don't think my lack of communication means I have grown any less fond of you.

We are still very much alive. God has blessed us incredibly, and it is hard to know where to begin catching you up, but I'll try.

First of all, we want you to know that if you ever get over to Canaan, we would love to put you up and show you the area. There are a lot of fascinating historical attractions—from the ruins of Sodom and Gomorrah to the giant oak tree at Mamre where my grandfather conducted his business. Anyway, consider yourself invited. We have comfortable guest tents and are happy to share them any time. The weather here is usually fantastic. Land is a little dry, but it is cheap and very available.

As some of you know, a few years back I was living in Haran in order to be near Uncle Laban and to further my education. It was more rewarding than I could have ever imagined: in fourteen years, I not only made some *huge* breakthroughs in my genetic research with cattle and sheep—I managed to acquire two gorgeous wives! How I found time for everything, I'll never know!

My sheep and cattle weren't the only reproducers: my wives and, oh, yes, my two lovely concubines were very busy—make that me, too. ☺ We now have twelve sons and some daughters also. Believe me, our string of racing camels are *very* popular and rather over-worked around here. The mess tent is also a popular hangout. Our kitchen servants can hardly keep enough lambs on the spit to feed this tribe.

I've been working out lately, trying to keep the old body trim and all. It sure paid off recently during an unexpected wrestling match. Unbelievable, but I actually wrestled an angel and came out the winner! Got a new name out of the deal—Israel, and a promise that I would become the father of many nations. (Note: I've been doing *my* part to fulfill this!)

Another highlight was the fantastic reunion with my brother Esau whom I hadn't seen in years. What a great time we had reminiscing about our boyhood.

My daughters are the envy of all around here because of their great beauty. Dinah even received a proposal from the son of the Shechem, the local king. Seems like every time I turn around, I'm negotiating with or chasing a suitor off—you know how fathers need to protect their daughters!

My sons have grown up strong and healthy and many of them have taken positions in the family business. In fact, not long ago they surprised me with quite a coup—a sort of leveraged buyout, I suppose. They managed to completely annex a nearby town (used to belong to Shechem) without the loss of a single penny to us. It turned out to be a wealthy little place and we managed to greatly increase our property holdings and livestock. We even gained a lot of free domestic and field help out of the deal. Their creativity amazes me.

I guess our son Joseph tops all. This year he's been promoted to a new high, even for our family. He moved to Egypt some years ago. Really likes it there. Loves the urban life and has always been a sharp dresser and creative thinker, so he's found himself a special niche over there. He holds the highest political position in the country and is second only to the Pharaoh himself. But he's never forgotten his roots and has really been generous to us. In fact, you might pray about this; we may be moving to Egypt ourselves.

We really praise God for all his blessings and hope that your year has been as fruitful as ours.

Stay in touch and remember you're welcome anytime—even in Egypt. Shalom.

Your Cousin, Jacob

JACOB'S ANNUAL CHRISTMAS LETTER, VERSION TWO

Dear Family and Friends,

I know it's been awhile. I apologize. I've hesitated to write as things haven't gone the way I'd hoped they would over the past year. But as things are now, I may as well bring you up to date on some of what's transpired. If nothing else, you might pray for us.

As you may already know, some years ago I had to flee for my life as I tricked Esau, my twin brother, into selling me his birthright for reasons I won't go into here.

I ended up in Haran, staying at my Uncle Laban's and working for him. I fell in love with Rachel, his younger daughter. He promised her to me if I worked seven years for him. I was so in love it only seemed like a few days. But he swindled me, for on our marriage night, who should he send me all veiled and smelling of lilies? Rachel's older sister, Leah. It was dark in the tent, so it wasn't until morning that I discovered, too late, that I'd been had. I was so angry.

Of course Laban was only too happy to renegotiate another seven-year contract for Rachel, to which I agreed.

For fourteen years I worked and ended up with nothing but two wives who fought constantly and two concubines, whom they played off against me, and about a dozen sons to provide for. Laban's worth must have risen 500 percent under my management, but he paid me nothing for all my effort.

Finally, I went to him and offered a deal—if he would let me have all the spotted livestock (which were pretty rare at the time) I would consider that my pay. I used every bit of knowledge and a little sorcery to help us out and, well, it was unbelievable: pretty soon females of every sort were popping off spotted and striped babies. Almost overnight I became a wealthy man.

Then one night God came to me telling me to move back to Canaan. Seeing that my affairs had taken a turn for the better, I decided to go ahead. I knew I would have to keep it a secret from Laban as he might try to stop me or even kill me, so I left without even saying au revoir.

On the journey back to Canaan, I was attacked by an angel or possibly God himself. I wrestled with him all night until I thought I would die. Somehow, and despite the fact that he permanently injured my hip, I was able to extract a promise from him about making me the father of many nations.

I was dreading the reunion with my brother Esau. In fact, I was so afraid to meet him that, as we approached the home country, I set it up so that flock after flock (a lot of them gifts for Esau) and herd after herd would pass ahead of me, followed by my wives and children and lastly me. I know it sounds cowardly, but I hoped he would be assuaged. He was polite, but not very friendly. Something of a sorrow to me.

About this time, and after so many years of trying, Rachel died while giving birth to her second son, Benjamin. I was inconsolable. She was always my favorite. That was soon followed by the death of my old father, Isaac.

As my sons grew, they seemed always on the brink of violence and vengeance. It broke out in a devastating way after they found out that one of my daughters, Dinah (who *is* beautiful) had been seduced by a local fellow. They orchestrated the most cruel revenge. They pretended to agree Dinah could marry him if all the men got circumcised. It's one thing to have this done when you're eight days old, you know what I mean? While the men lay around nursing their members, my sons killed them, carried off all the wealth and livestock, and enslaved the women and children. There was nothing I could do about it. They've always been headstrong and unmanageable. Dinah hasn't spoken to us since.

As if I didn't have enough sorrow, the boys had always been jealous of their brother Joseph, who was Rachel's oldest son. I admit I favored him a little, but they didn't need to do what they did. My sons sold him into slavery in Egypt and brought his beautiful coat home all stained in blood. They lied to me. They claimed they found it and that he must have been killed by a wild animal. You can't imagine how I felt.

Lately we have suffered from the most severe famine. I believe we have lost nearly everything. But with it has come the only good news in years. After all this time, I have learned Joseph is alive. He's in Egypt holding a very powerful position in the government. We found out when my sons went down there looking to buy food.

I hardly dare hope. They say Joseph wants us to move there and live with him. They say he has forgiven them for what they did to him. I only pray this might be so. It would bring me such great happiness.

Please pray for us as I am old and we are packing for a long journey. Pray that God would give me strength and show us mercy. We are in deep need.

Shalom, J. Israel

It's remarkable that in Scripture, God never gives us a disinfected view of his people. The second letter is closer to the unvarnished account of Jacob in Genesis. The first letter is more like a typical annual Christmas letter which glows in an artificial light. Jacob was a man with many flaws and I'm thankful to know it. If I had written Genesis, I'm sure I would have been tempted to give a more sanitized version.

Despite the sadness and sin in Jacob's life, the book of Hebrews includes him as a man of great faith, one who understood God's promises, and who, at the end of his life, was still worshiping the Lord. God doesn't shrink from this real man whose troubles are written down for all the centuries to see; God refers to himself as the God of Abraham, Isaac, *and Jacob.* It's one of the things that makes me love Christianity. Who else would dare to claim a scoundrel like Jacob? Down through the centuries this name—"the God of Jacob"—has become a source of comfort for all who read his story.

This gives me the courage to report on our lives with a little more honesty when I communicate with others. We want to share good news and joy—that's what the season is about, but only in part. When we admit failures and sorrow, we stand with a vast company of fellow sufferers along with Jacob, King David, and Mary. For those of us who don't live perfect, trouble-free lives, this is godly comfort and truly "Good News." We are not alone in a dark and broken world. God is pleased to claim us as his own.

DOWN THE RABBIT HOLE

SUMMER 2005

"Are you from the Unitarian Church?"

A small, dark-haired woman drinking a soy latte and holding a copy of *Enlightenment* magazine smiled encouragingly at me. Others seated around the table at Dunn Brothers Coffee stared at me and waited. I'd only been there thirty seconds before I realized this would *not* be a discussion I controlled. I'd never been mistaken for a Unitarian. Did I look like a Unitarian? I wasn't wearing a batik jersey dress with Kokopelli on the front.

The evening before I'd seen the movie *What The Bleep Do We Know?!* with our small group from church. It had been featured as part of a local film festival. Although it isn't a great work of art, it brings up all the big questions about life and meaning. It asks them in your face and then gives you a set of postmodern answers. We stayed up late wondering how many of our neighbors and colleagues believed or acted on these ideas—and if they did, how we could engage them in conversation and communicate Christian beliefs to them.

Before we parted, one of our group mentioned that the next afternoon at Dunn Brothers Coffee there was going to be a public discussion on *What the Bleep* sponsored by the film festival. I decided to join them. Life can be way too sheltered in our climate-controlled Christian community; I needed a shot of live, uncensored non-Christians talking about life and ideas. It could be a Saint Paulish Mars Hill spy-trip. I would listen, learn, and at the right moment, I could give a gorgeous presentation of the gospel.

What the Bleep Do We Know?! is a movie about quantum mechanics, sort of. My brain contains a file titled Quantum Mechanics, but it's empty—except for a scrap of corrupted information about atoms unexpectedly leaving their assigned places, or a particular atom being in several places at once. (This is a power every parent would like, but it's a power possessed only by children and atoms.) So, scientists tell us, if you deliberately focus on an atom and try to catch her doing this trick, she is standing still. And that is, like, just a tiny piece of a fascinating science with links to time, reality, origins, spirituality, and... truly, what the bleep do I know?

The movie is part documentary, part story, and part animation. Amanda, played by Marlee Matlin, finds herself in a weird, *Alice in Wonderland*-like experience when her daily, uninspired life literally begins to unravel, revealing the uncertain world of the quantum field hidden behind her normal, waking reality. Fourteen scientists and mystics are interviewed throughout the film and their ideas are woven together to emphasize the film's underlying concept of the inter-connectedness of all things. They serve as a kind of Greek chorus and introduce the Big Questions of Life as the story leads us down the "rabbit hole." Several of the experts mention that there appears to be a "Silent Observer" behind the energies of the universe, but most agree they don't know for certain what makes the universe run. At the conclusion, one of the experts, known as Ramtha, looks into the camera and tells us there is no way for humans to determine what is right or wrong, and that believing in a God who will judge or punish a person for what they have done is ridiculous, because everyone chooses their own path, their own reality. *That*, she says, *is the beginning of wisdom.*

Critics differed widely on the film's success. Peter Howell of the *Toronto Star* wrote that he thought the film had the year's most unfortunate title and was also the worst film of the year. Critic Susan Granger lauded the film describing it as provocative, and an opening to an entire world of knowledge and ideas.

What I didn't know that Sunday afternoon when I joined the film discussion was that this independent movie is the work of students of J.Z. Knight, who calls herself Ramtha. Ramtha is a 35,000 year-old wise man, who appeared in Knight's kitchen one afternoon in 1977. She's been channeling him ever since. Of the fourteen interviewees, a number either work for or teach in her School of Enlightenment. Others who don't work for her organization—as in the case of David Albert, professor and director of the Philosophical Foundations of Physics program at Columbia University was outraged when the film came out. He told *Popular Science*[1] that he had spent four hours patiently explaining why quantum mechanics had nothing to do with consciousness or spirituality. In the movie the filmmakers turned his views around 180 degrees.

For that afternoon discussion, I hadn't yet done this research. But even if I knew all there was to know about quantum physics and Transcendental Meditation, there's a limit to my capacity. However, my intellectual limitations aren't an excuse for never engaging with non-Christians unless it's in a controlled environment like a Bible study where there's no risk for me. It's more of a challenge to believe God is with me in a coffee shop when I'm missing my PhD, my research, and a brilliant mind.

I take heart from Jonathan, King Saul's son. When he was scouting a high tech Philistine military outpost, he was outgunned, outmanned, and in a suicidal position to attack (1 Sam. 14:1–23). But he said to his attaché, basically, "With God, the odds on winning don't matter, so why don't we do a little rock climbing and see what happens?" I love his armor-bearer's response: "I'm with you heart and soul!" No military strategist would have predicted the resulting disaster for the Philistines. That's reality in every dimension, including quantum mechanics: God controls the universe. He's also pleased to use people who aren't power brokers in any way, which means I'm a player. The gospel's power to save doesn't depend on my comprehension of physics or neopaganism. I can show up with my heart and soul even when it's a risky, blundering piece of rock climbing.

So, there were nine of us around the table and I was the lone stranger among them. It was instructive to remind myself that this is how a visitor to our Bible study might feel. The only person I knew was a friend who quietly slipped in beside me about halfway through the discussion. She observed everything, so I can't pretend to be the next Francis Schaeffer by reporting how great I was.

I wanted to remain anonymous, listen quietly, and scope out how hostile they'd be if they knew I was a Christian. I was barely seated with an Americano when, together, they focused on me: "When did you see the movie? How did you hear about it? How many times have you seen it? What did you think? Did you like it?"

I tried to evade, answering with a modest, "I really want to hear what you guys think of the movie." They totally ignored that, like they knew I was stonewalling. They insisted on knowing who I was. I told them, "I saw the movie the first time last night with a group of friends from our church." Nervously, I added, "We regularly get together to discuss movies, popular culture, and other things" (other things being the *Bible,* which I didn't say). That prompted another chorus of questions: "What did they think about it? Did they like it? Hey, are you from the Unitarian Church?"

The last question was delivered with such anticipation and preapproval, I felt a little ashamed dashing their hopes. I took a long, noisy sip of coffee. No one had ever confused me with a Unitarian. I've noticed that evangelicals generally despise Unitarians. "Why *bother?*" they say. "Just join the country club or the music guild, but don't *pretend* to be religious." At the same time I wondered: are we so isolated and insular that it's preposterous for me to be a Christian and yet be someone who takes questions of art and culture seriously?

Finally, I replied: "No. I'm a Presbyterian. Not from the big church, the little one over on 14th street. We thought the ideas in the movie were fascinating and talked for hours about how you know that you know, how to define reality, and how to describe the soul."

They looked extremely pleased with me, like I'd just given them deep muscle massage for free. I was among pagans, but I could see they were interesting and smart. So with the next breath, I prudently admitted I hadn't the slightest capacity for discussing molecular biology, quantum physics, hormone receptors, or any other philosophical explanations for the nature of existence.

Everyone assured me they weren't experts either, then talked about how much they loved the movie. And how at first the main character, Amanda, was afraid of the interconnected reality that existed on an atomic level. Was reality just the reaction of her hormones on her cell receptors? Was it some other mysterious energy that lay beyond her senses? Amanda was hoping to find answers before she had a nervous breakdown. One of her most painful questions was why her husband was unfaithful from the beginning, including the very day of their wedding. The group thought his infidelity was the result of Amanda's choices whether she recognized it or not. It was merely the path she had to travel to finally reach peace.

Huge pause. Did I need to assert, "This makes no sense. Her husband was a jerk, he hurt her deeply because—label it whatever you want—we are creatures who instinctively recognize betrayal and injustice. There are absolutes. This is one of them: a groom doesn't ever, *ever* get to screw around on his wedding day. So why are you making *her* responsible for this pain?" Instead, I made myself very quiet and, so I wouldn't roll my eyes, stared down my nose into my coffee mug.

A thin man with an unruly mop of long, gray hair and his shoulder in a sling seemed to sense my conflict. He looked at me with rheumy eyes and offered, "The only time I experience happiness and freedom from pain is when I meditate. I get into that zone where there is nothing. Where the mind is just blank. I do this every day." He looked so sweet. There were nods of sympathy around the table.

The cheerful woman, the one holding *Enlightenment* magazine, said, "You see? He"—the thin man—"is creating his own reality! He has options! We all have choices that enable us to choose our paths in spite of pain or what others do to us. To do that you go 'inner,' inside yourself where you find your own gods."

At this point, some would loudly dispute this. Only Jesus Christ is *Lord*. Although that is my belief with every atom of my heart, a microsecond's reflection told me saying that wouldn't convert them. In fact, it would probably only succeed in alienating them.

Instead, I summoned courage and asked, "I'd like to understand what you mean by 'gods.' I think of God as a being outside myself." A lady in a purple sweater and a white dandelion head told me, "Well, god is you. It's your peptides and hormones. It's a power inside you that causes you to do certain things."

From the movie, I remembered a bizarre animation of hormones pouring out of an obese man's body, making him stand over a table at a wedding reception, stuffing food into his mouth until it dribbled down his front and bloated his belly. No one approved of this behavior. This seemed inconsistent. The onlookers criticized the man for behaving in a socially unacceptable way, while still believing that his hormones controlled his actions and that he couldn't help acting as he did. How could they place more value on certain behaviors when, by their own logic, they shouldn't have a problem with whatever one's hormones choose to do? Or with whatever happens? No one seemed to notice this.

The lady in purple continued, "You have the power to control your response on the receptors of each and every one of your cells. We have options. We can choose our own path and we become whatever god we want to be."

Debbie, a young social worker at the end of table, said, "I liked the scientists in the movie, especially the one in front of the fireplace who explained that the brain doesn't necessarily recognize reality. For the brain to see something, like, say, a clipper ship on the sea... well, it can't see a clipper ship on the sea if it's never seen one before, can it? What we see, what we know, is conditioned by culture and experience, so if we've never seen a ship before and let's say we're a Native American standing on the beach and Columbus is pulling into port, the ship doesn't exist for the brain."

I felt sad not to offer a more compelling response. "But if you can't see the ship because the brain has no categories for it, then how can we even conceive the question humans ask all the time: *what is that?* Do you think this means reality can't exist outside our own ability to perceive it? And if reality is only imagined, how would we explain the viruses brought by Columbus, which killed so many Native Americans? Were they real or not?"

A man in a flannel shirt and blue jeans said, "I'm a hunter." (This intrigued me. Was he allowed to admit that?) "And, once, years ago I took a friend into the woods. He'd never been hunting before. He couldn't see anything. Couldn't see game at all even though it was right in front of us! Only when I helped him, pointed to a deer, could he see it. His brain couldn't see because, well, he hadn't the experience. His eyes saw, but didn't *really* see because he had no categories in which to place it."

Someone responded, "And we can't judge what's right or what's wrong for another person. It's personal choice."

This seemed so random, I changed the subject. "So, who is the Silent Observer they talk about in the movie?"

Debbie answered: "The Silent Observer is what I call my soul. I'm not good at listening to it. My soul observes what I know and wants me to take a chance on what I don't know, a chance for a better path. But I don't make that choice because I'm comfortable with the misery I already know. And life has been pretty miserable lately." (She began to cry, and the person next to her kindly put a hand on her arm.) "Although it's only in a small way, there's a natural goodness in my soul, deep down—something all people have. In that goodness, I move toward healing and try to help others become aware of that goodness in them so they can be healed. In this way, I have hope that the world too, will be healed."

Here were people sincerely trying to make sense of a world of suffering, trying so hard to do what was right. Would they suddenly see the freedom hidden in the gospel's verdict if I told them, "All have sinned and fallen short of the glory of God?" (Rom. 3:23) Would they understand that if, indeed, our path to salvation depends on our ability to think positively, meditate, control hormone receptors, listen to the soul—then aren't we merely committing ourselves to a new law, a works-righteousness system that can never be kept? Isn't it obvious what we all need is a cosmic, divine, mysterious rescue by a perfect and powerful source outside ourselves? No, they wouldn't understand. But you need to start somewhere. I relate to honesty and humility and thought perhaps they would, too.

I finally said to Debbie, "I admire your spirit and your desire to be good. To be honest, most of the time, I'm ashamed because my natural inclinations don't move toward Good at all. If the practice of Goodness is left to me, I'm ruined, and so is the world. Take the smallest, most insignificant thing—I'm naturally selfish and I channel"—probably the wrong word to use in that group—"anger hate, impatience. I don't think peptides and hormones entirely explain this inner motion toward evil. Just the other night I was so completely, disproportionately angry because this friend took the wrong way to our destination. It took all my power not to yell and grab the steering wheel. I vowed never to be in a car with this person again unless I was driving—all because it made us two minutes late. So if we depend on *me* to improve humanity, we're doomed. God, help me." And I brought both hands up and touched my forehead with my fingers in a gesture of frustration.

It looked like a total failure to connect because the cheerful woman triumphantly shouted, "You see? You are unconsciously appealing to your inner god with that motion. You did *this!*" (She copied my hand movement.) Everyone laughed and nodded, having caught me, a Christian, in a pagan motion indicating my "inner god." I had no idea the gesture had a particular meaning to them.

Dismayed, I protested, "No, no, no! I do *that* too, on my knees, my hands up, crying help with all my heart to God in heaven." I gestured, both hands in the air, palms up. Still, they laughed, and I did, too.

The cheerful woman concluded that the more of us who determine together to change, the more we truly *can* change—ourselves, even the world. "Think of the study," she said, "done on violent crime in the DC area in 1993. For two weeks, four thousand transcendental meditation experts meditated on peace, and the crime rate decreased by 18 percent" The thin man sounded hopeful: "So, we could have moved the tectonic plates, stopped the tsunami that hit Indonesia if enough of us meditated?" Many of them nodded, "Yes!"

Then I heard a quiet voice. A tall woman (one of the organizers of the film festival) directly across from me who hadn't spoken the entire time softly said, "Bullshit." I clearly heard her, but others were asking, what did she say, what did she say? She gently repeated it: "Bull"—pause—"shit." Equal weight on both words.

It was a shock, a verbal tsunami. Everyone was silent for a minute. I began to quietly laugh. Others joined in for other reasons, I suppose. The two-hour discussion was over.

One member of the group was a writer and invited me to get in touch with her. She wants to talk more about ideas of spirituality and mystery. But I'd definitely like to call the tall, one-word woman. Her summary was brilliant.

I need these encounters. My neighbors are real people battling pain, broken relationships, political tyranny, injustice, and natural disasters. Their efforts to find peace disarmed my reluctance to listen to them, sitting there, as I did, without scripted answers. I understand more clearly their dead-end paths to salvation. No one wins heaven if in the end you are left on your own to fight the war against evil within and without. You can invoke spiritual power all you want, but in the end, humans always lose. Even as a Christian, I'm familiar with this struggle. I've lost many times. The perfect beauty of the gospel is that God, in Christ, entirely gave himself to win that battle for us. That's what I wanted to tell them, but sometimes you only get half a shot. Perhaps their next encounter will be with Jonathan, and the Philistines of their lives will fall left and right. I pray so.

JOY IN UNEXPECTED PLACES

WINTER 2005

One reason I think God made children is because they're gifted at creating the surprise of joy in the midst of some pretty startling circumstances. Jeremy Huggins once reported on his blog *Junkmail For Blankets* that he was visiting a friend whose "two-year-old girl vomited all over the table where I was sitting. She looked down at the vomit, looked up at me, laughed, and said, 'Jeremy, I frowed up.'" Jeremy is not a father. Which, strangely, increased the irony and the humor of this, don't you think?

Although I can't trump a child having spontaneous joy over such a strange thing, I can recall a few random stories that might amuse us for a moment or two.

My Aunt Beatty Frolander, who was as Swedish as a meatball, fondly called my mother a "dumb Svede," even though Mom is not a blonde, and even though last fall she shot a buck from her bathroom window. (This doesn't mean as her daughter I'm a crack shot or as good-looking, but it does make me Scandinavian, which means I get to tell my people's jokes.)

At a farmer's market last fall, Denis and I overheard a grizzled Norwegian tell a joke to a circle of old guys who slapped their thighs in appreciation. Sven, Ole, and his wife, Lena, were ice fishing on a little lake in Minnesota. After they fished awhile, Ole asks Lena if she'd walk across the lake over there to Johnson's bait shop and buy him some beef jerky, don't you know? She says, "Ya, I s'pose I will. Do you have any money?" Ole says, "No, but you can just put it on my account there, then." They watched her walk about half a mile across the ice, and Sven finally says, "Ole, how come you didn't give her some cash, I know you got some there in your pocket?" Ole replied, "I didn't know how thick the ice was." (Don't feel too sorry for Lena. She gets back at Ole plenty of times.)

Irony is, as English majors know, the incongruity between what actually happens and what might be expected to happen, especially when this disparity seems absurd or laughable. I especially enjoy irony in someone else's life, like

Jeremy and the vomit. I'm not as keen on it in my own, but it does happen. This is a story dedicated to the incongruity of God's mercy applied to who I am, which is also a sort of irony mixed with joy.

In a large room decorated with construction cones, tool belts, and key-chains with tiny replicas of hammers and screwdrivers as party favors, women sat around tables eating fabulous desserts, and, I suppose, contemplating the metaphor that surrounded them. *Extreme Makeovers* was the title for this women's event. Husbands and sons, awkward in the role of waiting tables, threaded between us with carafes of coffee and tea. I nervously waited to be introduced as the main speaker for this church's gathering of friends and neighbors.

Before I spoke, Sylvia (not her real name) was on the program to give a kind of summary of what God has done in her life. Christians call it a "testimony." Sylvia, a diminutive young woman with beautiful eyes, stood behind the podium and told us about the fifteen lost years of her life. It began with a little bulimia and ended with her as a 68-pound anorexic and an abuser of alcohol and prescription drugs. Like addictions will do, they demanded everything from her, not only her body weight, but a few small items like her heart, liver, friends, family, and husband.

All she had left was this tiny, little shred of life when her younger brother came to tell her that he, too, was finally giving up on her like everyone else. He told her, "You've ruined your life. You've ruined our family. When are you ever gonna change?" Assuming she wouldn't, he sat beside her, crying for a long time and then left without hope. She'd been confronted many times, but something about her little brother's sadness completely broke her heart, and she marks that time as the turning point of her life. That night she threw everything down before God and cried out, "Help me. I need you. I want you."

That was two years ago and the beginning of Christ's remarkable redemption of her life. We sat at the same table together; I met her mother and her grandmother. Her husband was there too; he was out in the hall with their "miracle" baby in his arms, a round-faced, laughing little girl. He paced back and forth outside the auditorium, praying for his wife. As Sylvia got up, I saw her mom squeeze her hand and say, "You'll do fine." And she did. Sylvia cried from the moment she began her talk until she ended with this passage from Jeremiah: "I know the plans I have for you, declares the Lord, plans to prosper you and not to harm you, plans to give you hope and a future" (Jer. 29:11).

After this beautiful story of amazing grace, it was my turn. It took about one second for me to realize that this would be like the talented Emmylou Harris opening for an unknown, unheard of act. What I wanted to do was praise God, buy her CD, and go home. But I'd driven 250 miles to be there, and they'd also put me up in a very nice hotel suite with a nifty bedside radio and an ice maker *in the room!* I knew I had to face these women. So as they dabbed their eyes, I plunged ahead with a confession about why I probably shouldn't even be there. Then they could go home if they wanted, since they'd already eaten their dessert and heard Sylvia. The absurdity of this is that for a Christian my age, it would seem the whole situation should have been, well, avoidable.

Last summer in the space of a few weeks, I received more invitations to speak than I had in the previous two years altogether. I was beginning to wonder if God was sending me a message. Like, you're an okay person even if you're a little discouraged and haven't cleaned the vegetable drawer in the refrigerator for six months. It's true that most of the invitations were not destinations, unless you've heard of Onalaska, WI, or Hinckley, MN. I just wasn't up to adding a speaking itinerary to my already anxious, over-wrought life. So I turned them all down except for this one, which I accepted quite by accident, though God may think otherwise.

I was having a weak moment as I listened to the message on the answering machine left by my friend, Lisa, asking about the possibility of speaking at her church, when the mail arrived with one of my favorite clothing catalogs. I usually throw it away. But this time I said to my husband, as I leafed through, "If I find an outfit I like, I'll say yes to this invitation." It'd been three years since I'd actually shopped for anything special. I won't mention which catalog because if I say it was Kmart you might think I'm cheap and sleazy. But if I say Neiman Marcus, you'll wonder how I could afford it, which I can't.

I was stunned to find something I really liked. I even lapsed into Minnesotan, yelling, "Oh, fer cue-it!" Then I laughed, and looking at the ceiling, I announced, "I was only joking about accepting." Then I felt so wicked. I only hoped God had a sense of humor, so to be on the safe side, I decided I had to say yes to this invitation. You immediately see the problem: this wasn't because I cared about people or wanted to be used of God to encourage others.

The irony deepened when I learned the theme for the evening was *Extreme Makeover, Inside Edition*, and how we are often tempted to live as if the most important thing is how we look on the outside. I should have just bailed. But I had already ordered that great-looking dress. Somehow, in my talk that night, I managed to segue from the introductory confession into the idea that the central reality of our lives needs to be Jesus and that anything else we place there, even if it's a good thing, will eventually break our hearts. Which lately has been at the core of what I continue to learn about the Christian life.

Wherever Denis or I speak, we are usually invited to put out free samples of our ministry's publications and a sign-up sheet for our mailing list. At the end of that evening in Sioux Falls, SD, most of my samples were left on the table. Of the 200 guests, two people signed up for our mailing list. By human measures, this event was possibly one of my most humiliating failures. But, of course, you can never be certain what God might do with the material he has to work with.

One good thing: I'm still here, and not so dull-witted I can't appreciate the irony of my own existence. It isn't divine neglect, as if God failed to notice what I was doing or saying. No, he sees me very well, and it is strictly a matter of God's loving kindness that I haven't been snuffed out. A week later I heard from a young woman who wrote she was deeply moved by my talk. Discouraged with her church and the youth group she was leading, she had been on the verge of quitting. Somehow what I said touched a chord and she was willing to believe God was still present and working through her even if she wasn't seeing evidence right then.

During most of the drive home, I listened to one song that's not from a Christian group, as far as I know. Often, unaware, unbeknownst to the composer, a song can become a hymn that helps you find God in unusual places. I heartily sang Reindeer Section's "You Are My Joy" from the CD *Son of Evil Reindeer*. The words are mostly a repetition of the title, which normally makes me think the songwriter was either in a trance or pressed the loop button too many times. But it works here as a lengthy meditation. I thought of my desire to make Jesus central to all my reality and that if he were with me, I'd dedicate the song to him, because after all I've eaten and drunk in this life, he is still the best thing, my joy. Then, I thought, if he were with me, he might sing this to *me*. The notion of us being his joy is from Hebrews 12, where we are told he endured the cross for the "joy set before him" (v. 2). What he did not have before the cross was us. So I continued to sing, "You are my joy, you are my joy, you are my jo-oh-oh-ee" for both of us.

I find no irony or cynicism in this. There is only surprise and joy that we could be so beloved. And so, we sincerely wish you a very merry Christmas. May you always be surprised by joy in unexpected places.

CALM DOWN

WINTER 2006

I've always thought of myself as intuitive because that is how I score on personality tests. It's supposed to bless me with clarity of perception in the subconscious world, but it seems doubtful that I put that intuition to very good use. If I did, wouldn't I be perceptive enough to avoid useless tests of rationally constructed logic? Consider the following.

There is this growing popularity of sudoku, the Japanese number puzzles, which at first I thought was just the fruit of poisonous minds—or at least ones without enough to do. Then they began appearing in our daily newspaper. After ignoring them for about seven months, I tried one and finished it in twelve minutes. I was so surprised and pleased with myself, I thought I might take that IQ test on mensa.org and find out if it cost anything to join them. The next night, as I was relaxing in my chair with the soundtrack from *Grizzly Man* softly playing and my husband quietly reading a seminary textbook, I tore out Tuesday's sudoku and almost finished it before bedtime.

After supper on Wednesday I began my third sudoku with jaunty confidence. Two-and-a-half hours later Denis begged me to please come to bed. I did, but I took it with me and worked on it for another hour without adding a single number. Only then did I notice five stars at the bottom of the puzzle with three of them shaded. A crack of light entered my darkened mind: Oh. This indicates difficulty factor. The one in my hand was a 3-star. The previous night's (with solution) was printed at the bottom; it had only been a 2-star. With logic gaining momentum despite intuition, it occurred to me that as the week goes by, the puzzles increase in difficulty sort of like the *New York Times* crosswords so that by the time you get to the weekend they're so punishing you want to pay your own way to New York, find the editor, and force him to eat iceberg lettuce and Velveeta cheese until he can give you an eight-letter-word for "rugged outdoor clothing." Carhartt! Idiot! As *anyone* north of Minneapolis would know. And I don't want to hear, my friend, how you can do it in ten minutes while blogging, writing a movie review, and flirting with the barista. By then I was crushed, in addition to feeling slightly crazy. But I rallied and told myself, "You've always despised logic, so why in the name of all your precious hormones don't you just intuit the solution? A few numbers should not defeat you."

Have you ever considered, even for one second, praying that God would help you finish a puzzle? Well. Okay. Maybe you haven't. But what about scoring a three-pointer from mid-court, or beating a red light? Or shooting a trophy buck? You know it's the same thing.

At 11:30 p.m. Denis raised an eyebrow at me and turned out the light on his side. I held the paper out for us to observe—it was covered with hundreds and hundreds of teeny, tiny numbers written in patterns, grids, and graphs. Suddenly, it was scary because there it was: *A Beautiful Mind*! Remember that scene from the movie when the door of John Forbes Nash's office opens and on every wall, floor to ceiling, are little papers with hand-written numbers, formulas and codes, and you suddenly understood how ill he is, even though he is a genius? This was my mind on paper and it was not well. I shrieked, threw the paper and pen across the room, and turned off the light.

In the dark I recalled a favorite psalm:

> My heart is not proud, O LORD,
> my eyes are not haughty;
> I do not concern myself with great matters
> or things too wonderful for me.
> But I have stilled and quieted my soul;
> Like a weaned child with its mother,
> Like a weaned child is my soul within me.
> O Israel, put your hope in the LORD
> both now and forevermore (Ps. 131).

Of course, sudoku is only a symptom—a metaphor of what's more generally wrong with me. As a mother I understand weaning a child. A baby has no idea why her mother made her stop doing her favorite thing in all the world. But in order to grow, she must give it up. Her mother doesn't love her any less. She still encircles her arms about her baby and looks at her with shining eyes. Finally the child quits her wriggling demand for milk and relaxes with her head on her mother's breast. Sometimes it takes weeks.

There's nothing wrong with solving sudoku puzzles. It's just that for the most part, I can't. In a similar way, I often try to fix things too great for me. I push and strain, trying to clean up the messes of life and am discouraged when I can't. Often I ask God exactly why he's not helping out a little here? But I am admonished by David to give up my demands. We must accept that if we minister and live in the real world, there will always be certain matters in life that escape human solution. They will not be resolved by efficient, practical minds or by intuitive insight either. I am redirected to quietness, to calming my soul. David turns away from inner conflict and adjusts his focus outward; he addresses his people, *O, Israel.* This is a place where we stand together in community, with the body of Christ, and we resolve to hope in the Lord forever and watch for glory to be revealed. We can never be certain of when or how God will appear as the One who is able to do "immeasurably more than all we ask or imagine" (Eph. 3:20).

The next day's paper had a 5-star sudoku—the most difficult. I looked at it and calmly said, "I will not do this to myself ever again." And I put it in the trash. I think that's being weaned? Sometimes it takes years, but slowly I bend my head to God's shoulder and rest—even as I rejoice that Jessica, who is a bright, diligent L'Abri helper, says 3x3s are so easy she needs to do 4x4s to be challenged *in the slightest.* Then she adds, "Sudoku is something I can do without thinking at all, the answers are just so obvious." That is a matter almost "too wonderful for me" to understand.

The next night as I was about to fall asleep, Denis mentioned that we need to save more money. Then, he got a pained, far-away look in his eye like any minute he was going to excrete a kidney stone or something. It made me a little nervous. But when he said we needed to make some repairs on the house, I panicked. I'm usually the one who keeps a list of the parts of our house looking slummy and downtrodden. Like the stairwell, which fortunately, I can now ignore because it's so high I've been able to train myself not to look up at the plaster dangling off the ceiling in large flakes or worry about them lacerating my scalp if they fall when the front door slams. As long as the dishwasher is loaded properly and I don't leave too many blankets flung about the living room, Denis is fairly content to ignore the house; it suits me fine that he leaves the painting and repairs to me. So I held my breath and tried to imagine what was so bad he wanted to save money for it. I tried to keep my voice level.

"So what repairs did you have in mind?"

I was hoping it was just the bathroom window, which we already agreed needs to be replaced because it no longer rolls in tight against the frame. When it was stuck a couple of summers ago, I stripped the threads of the handle by gripping it with both hands and cranking as hard as I could. Now you can see a tiny strip of skylight all around it if you look closely at the edge. And worse, you can feel cold air pour into the shower when you stand there in the morning, waiting for the blast of hot water to save you. Anyway, that window is old and

A leak in the attic destroyed boxes of books.

warped—it's one of those Andersen awning windows, so it can't be completely my fault. We should buy Marvin windows, not just out of loyalty to our son, Jerem, who works for them, but because they make the very best windows in the whole world. However, they cost that much, too.

We had a man from Larson out for an estimate last week. He's so skilled at what he does. Just stood in our bathtub, whipped out his measuring tape, squinted his eye, and said, "$850." Just like that. When we hesitated over triple thermal-pane glass he said, "Okay, a hundred dollars less, but you won't want to go cheaper than that. Er, I guess a guy could save a little more with a slider instead of a roll-out."

It wasn't the window that was bothering Denis after all. He told me, sotto voce, that before the L'Abri conference in mid-February, he'd gone up to the attic where we store boxes of his out-of-print book, *The Rest of Success.* A number of years ago the publisher let us buy up remainders for very cheap. I don't mean to get sidetracked. But do you see the irony of that title? *The Rest of Success: What the World Didn't Tell You About Having it All*? Still, we're lucky to have this big attic on the third floor of our house that holds so much stuff it's going to kill our kids when we die, because they're going to stand up there wondering *why* I saved those lampshades. *Because*. I'll tell you now: they're antique 1930s flapper-girl bedroom lampshades, and could be worth a lot of money. Probably not enough to repair the roof.

Anyway, up in the attic, Denis noticed two full boxes of books were completely soaked with water. WHAT?! I wanted to scream. For many thousands, we just had our roof *replaced* five years ago! I needed to breathe into a paper bag.

Denis tried to calm me down: "It's winter. No rain right now. We'll wait and I'll go up there and try to see where it's coming in the next time it rains."

"Are you kidding? This is Minnesota! Have you not noticed the two inches of rain we got, due to global warming, in early January? Or the snow that's fallen and melted about twenty times this winter instead of remaining on the ground until Memorial Day?"

I stared at the ceiling. *The Rest of Success* boxes are sitting right above us. I couldn't stand this breach in the very roof over our heads. It was like being told you have a mushroom growing out of your foot and the doctors will keep an eye on it until it begins giving off spores and shows signs of spreading up your calf, at which point they'll see if they can remove it. Of course, by then it will be too late and you will die.

I thought of two things I think we need. New shoes because, speaking of feet, my heel is hurting, which, when I googled it, Dr. Footdoctor said was plantar fasciitis; oh great. But far more costly, we need a new car because how long can our ten-year-old Taurus keep driving across country? I suppose I can keep on sitting in a seat that is so custom molded to my rear, it has sunk to the floorboards. I can keep on slamming the glove box shut. So what if it spontaneously falls open on my knees about five times per mile? It's too much to ask when the roof needs fixing.

For some mysterious reason, the psalm that scrolled across our compromised ceiling that night was both comforting and beautiful.

> Blessed are those you choose
> and bring near to live in your courts!
> We are filled with the good things of your house,
> of your holy temple.
> You answer us with awesome deeds of righteousness,
> O God our Savior,
> The hope of all the ends of the earth
> and of the farthest seas,
> Who formed the mountains by your power,
> having armed yourself with strength,
> Who stilled the roaring of the seas,
> the roaring of their waves, and the turmoil of the nations.
> Those living far away fear your wonders;
> Where morning dawns and evening fades
> you call forth songs of joy (Ps. 65).

By his Word and his unfailing provision year after year, I am utterly convinced of God's care for his people and of our ultimate destination. But I am convicted by lack of joy. There is a haiku feeling to part of the psalm—a powerful simplicity that condenses and intensifies the presence of God everywhere on earth.

> Where morning dawns
> And evening fades
> You call forth songs
> Of joy.

Farther than my eye can see, horizon to horizon, if we listen, we can hear God, coaxing us, inviting us to sing. Sufjan Stevens is one who hears songs of joy. (Sufjan's brilliant, creative music defies categories and is not found on the praise music scene.) He completely redeems what for me was an (I'm sorry) annoying old hymn. With banjo and simple vocals, so quiet, so profound, he sings "Come Thou Fount." I didn't mean to cry, to be taken by joy with a hymn I knew so well and formerly resented in my childhood. Every word of every verse came back unbidden.

> Come thou fount of every blessing, tune my heart to sing thy grace.
> Streams of mercy never ceasing call for songs of loudest praise.
> Teach me some melodious sonnet sung by flaming tongues above.
> Praise the mount I'm fixed upon it, mount of thy unchanging love.[1]

It's not as though Psalm 65 or "Come Thou Fount" repairs our roof or heals my friend's body which is being hijacked by cancer. I know that. It is meant to give sorely needed hope and perspective. It invites us to look beyond the confines of our own lives and be assured that, even if it's the end of a particular chapter of life, or of life itself, it is simply not the end of the story. Now and then we catch glimmers of another dimension all around us, a stream in the desert, a child snatched from danger, a song of joy. Sometimes in small ordinary ways, we experience the presence of God, as in the ability to get out of bed in the morning and keep our children alive. Other times we know for certain in the way a particular thing has fallen out, by its timing and our lack of control over it, that we've witnessed an unusual gift of grace.

In her book, *Julie & Julia*, author Julie Powell writes about how she decided to make *all* 524 recipes in Julia Child's *Mastering the Art of French Cooking* in one year and blog about it. I persevered to the end of the book to find this incredible acknowledgement on the last page, from someone who is at once talented, profane, and pretty far from God (possibly).

> Julia taught me what it takes to find your way in the world. It's not what I thought it was. I thought it was all about—I don't know, confidence or will or luck. Those are all some good things to have, no question. But there's something else, something that these things grow out of.
>
> It's joy.
>
> I know, I know—it's truly an obnoxious word, isn't it? Even typing it makes me cringe. I think of either Christmas cards or sixty-something New Agey women in floppy purple hats. And yet it's the best word I can think of for the heady, nearly violent satisfaction to be found in the text of Julia's first book. I read her instructions for making béchamel sauce, and what comes throbbing through is that here is a woman who has found her way.
>
> ... I didn't understand for a long time, but what attracted me to MtAoFC was the deeply buried aroma of hope and discovery of fulfillment in it. I thought I was using the Book to learn to cook French food, but really I was learning to sniff out the secret doors of possibility.[2]

Julie Powell precisely identifies our postmodern fear of joy. We're just cynical enough to think exhibitions of happiness will make us seem simple-minded, unsophisticated. And if we can't be rich or sexy we sure hope we can be profound.

So, I'm none of these things. But as it happens, I can cook, and oddly enough, it seems to be one of my songs of joy. Which means, give me an oven and a recipe for German beef short ribs and in three hours they'll smell so good Denis will emerge from his office, insisting he needs to eat them in the middle of the afternoon. I totally sent him away, because I planned to make mashed potatoes and sauerkraut to go with them. *Gloria Dei.*

REFLECTIONS ON WORK

FALL 2007

> Lord, let me know clearly the work which You are calling me to do in life. And grant me every grace I need to answer Your call with courage and love and lasting dedication to Your will.
>
> —Saint Meinrad[1]

Through the centuries many wise men and women have sought to help us sort out the joys, the troubles, and the questions our work brings.

LIFE IS SHORT. STAY AWAKE FOR IT

I'd guess Darcy has had enough of her company's slogan since sleep is what she'd most like right now. She is manager of our neighborhood Caribou Coffee and has become a friend. When we walked in the other day, she was slumped at a table pouring over shift schedules. Denis talked to her while I ordered from the twenty-two-year-old barista who leaned forward and whispered, "Darcy has worked for thirty-two days in a row, and today is her twenty-fifth birthday. I've been teasing her about being a quarter of a century old."

Meanwhile, Darcy was telling Denis she was finally forced to fire three problem-employees. One of them had threatened her harm, but it still made her sick to her stomach to do it. In the meantime she was working more hours to compensate for the loss. A good day now meant getting off for a couple hours, going home to nap, then getting right back to work. Stress was waking her at night so she started keeping a pad of paper beside the bed for when she thinks of something so she can write it down and try to leave it alone until morning.

Darcy is a graduate of the Culinary Institute of America. Managing a coffee shop was not what she dreamed of doing with her degree, but out of necessity she must work at a job that does not satisfy her creative gifts.

> It is not only prayer that gives God glory but work. Smiting on an anvil, sawing a beam, whitewashing a wall, driving horses, sweeping, scouring, everything gives God glory if being in his grace you do it as your duty. To go to communion worthily gives God great glory . . . but a man with a dung fork in his hand, a woman with a slop pail, give him glory too. He is so great that all things give him glory if you mean they should.
>
> —Gerard Manley Hopkins[2]

DITCH THE AGENDA

Martha and Mary. Classic working women from the Bible. Single, too. For years whenever I've heard someone (mostly men, sorry) teach about them—Mary is such the darling. Martha is *so* flawed. Who wouldn't know sitting at Jesus' feet is best, huh? Isn't it obvious Martha should have been sitting there listening at the feet of Jesus—where all you women should be?

No, it is not obvious. I like Martha. Mary annoys me. Martha was stressed because there were a lot of people milling about the house needing to be fed and cared for. Most of us need to be told it's okay to ditch our agendas and get out of the office, or the kitchen, or the whatever. But we should be told nicely and not like we're stupid for assuming someone needs to soak the barley and grate the cheese.

It isn't that Martha was intrinsically wrong as she prepared to serve guests. Jesus served in many ways and places, including feeding thousands of people in giant picnics. This firmly establishes that hospitality—wherever it is practiced—pleases God.

But think about it. If Jesus, maker of heaven and earth, was telling Martha "your work doesn't need to be done right this minute," then without a doubt, it's okay to abandon your agenda and choose to really be present with someone, especially when the Son of God is sitting on your couch. Jesus' exact words were, "Martha, Martha, you are worried and upset about many things, but only one thing is needed" (Luke 10:41). He acknowledges her stress, releases her from it, and in that moment redirects her to join the others in listening to what he was teaching. Hospitality was not to consume or define her as a person. But it was more than this. Jesus released her from the cultural belief that defined a successful—even a desirable—woman of her day.

This is still countercultural. The question that should be considered is: When is it proper for us to set aside our work duties? When something more important overrules them? When do we serve, when do we sit, when do we listen?

I read John 11 this morning. When they heard that Jesus was coming, both sisters were in deep grief after their brother Lazarus had died. This time it was

Martha who went to him first. There on the path outside her home, they stopped for an intimate conversation.

I can't get over how tender Jesus was with women, how he treated them with dignity and how often he told them things never heard before—things not even the disciples or theologians knew. That day he told Martha the seventh "I Am" of the Gospel of John. (You know how Bible scholars love numbers and call seven the perfect number? This was the seventh proclamation establishing Jesus as God, the great I AM of the Old Testament. How perfect is that?) He told Martha: "I am the resurrection and the life. He who believes in me will live, even though he dies . . . . Do you believe this?" (John 11:25, 26).

Martha answered, giving the first clear confession of Christ in the Gospel of John, saying, "Yes, Lord, I believe that you are the Christ, the Son of God, who was to come into the world." (v. 27)

I love her. I hope to talk to her one day. She makes me want to pray for the wisdom to know what must be done versus what to let go so I can be like Mary, ready to participate when something more important arrives. Martha also helps me realize that although I may not get it right the first time, that doesn't mean I can't learn to adjust my priorities.

DAY AFTER DAY

Leonard Cohen died in 2016, but he is still celebrated for his poetry and music. With honesty, he reflected on his bad attitude toward work when he was a Buddhist monk for twelve years in the monastery on Mt. Baldy in California. He was required to care for the daily needs of his aging Zen master—dressing him, feeding him, walking him. He recounts this time:

> For many years I was known as a monk. I shaved my head and wore robes and got up very early. I hated everyone, but acted generously and no one found me out. My reputation as a ladies' man was a joke, it caused me to laugh bitterly through the ten thousand nights I spent alone.
>
> —Leonard Cohen[3]

At times I have mistakenly envied the person who can leave this life behind with all its cares and responsibilities and join a monastery. Wouldn't it be wonderful to live in a place where all the details of daily life are prescribed, where I had nothing to do but follow the rules and meditate? Leonard Cohn affirms that just because we leave life behind for a place we thought would be idyllic, we can't escape ourselves. God created us to find satisfaction and purpose in finding and following his calling for our lives. John Calvin pulls me back to reality:

> It is an error to think that those who flee worldly affairs and engage in contemplation are leading an angelic life . . . we know that men were created to busy themselves with labor and that no sacrifice is more pleasing to God than when each one attends to his calling and endeavors well to live for the common good.
>
> —John Calvin[4]

THE PERILS OF WORK

Yesterday, Bill, my husband's brother-in-law, fell into the icy water while scalloping in Nantucket Bay. He managed to stay free of the ropes and avoid his skiff as the motor caused it to run in circles. He swam (in all his gear) to some nearby scallopers who saw his boat spinning, but didn't notice him. They moved closer and threw an anchor into his skiff to stop it. Instead, they sank it. He was finally rescued by the coast guard. Seasoned, skilled, wise fisherman—I don't know how this happened or how he survived. Neither does his wife. He's the last oceangoing fishing boat off Nantucket and has endured years of hard labor, surviving by supplementing their income with scalloping, bartering, and trading to keep on doing the work he loves.

He generously sends us packages of scallops that would altogether cost hundreds at the market. I sauté them in sizzling butter with a little chopped garlic and fresh thyme. When they are barely done, I remove them to a warm plate and add white wine and cream to the pan juices, reduce it, pour it over the scallops. Serve it with linguini and warm French bread. I think of what those ocean treasures cost Bill. Each sweet little piece dragged from the bottom of the bay with a long rake; pulled up hand-over-hand into the skiff; picked over with fingers numb from the cold, each shell painstakingly pared open with a knife; and the white muscle dropped into a bucket. The value of this catch is hard to imagine. I can barely eat this working man's glorious harvest, but then I do. His calling is to do the work of a fisherman.

> The place God calls you to is the place where your deep gladness and the world's deep hunger meet.
>
> —Frederick Buechner[5]

IN THE PRECIOUS MEANTIME

"While-U-Wait" the signs say. Just to sit under the bright light of the Jiffy Lube waiting room, sipping coffee from a plastic cup and leafing through a magazine while my car's fluids are being drained and exchanged, provides a rare sense of luxury. After all, I could be balancing my checkbook, grading my students' papers... Even in the space of "While-U-Wait" I feel I should be doing something else, something more.

Yet some of my most pleasurable moments have come when I allowed myself to sink into the feeling that something was taking place without—or in the aftermath of—my conscious intervention: to sit in the sun, reading a book, while under a damp towel and the shade of my chair a ball of dough rose in a bowl or six glass jars of hot milk thickened into yogurt, to lie on my back in the grass watching the clouds, my wet mop beside me, while inside the house the water shapes dried on clean, lemony wood floors. The precious "while" that follows when you have done your part, and surrendered the work of your hands to powers as great as sun, air, time.

—Noelle Oxenhandler.[6]

SMALL THINGS DO MATTER

When you see that you're making other things feel good, it gives you a good feeling, too.

The feeling inside sort of just happens, and you can't say this did it or that did it. It's the many little things. It doesn't seem that taking sweat-soaked harnesses off tired, hot horses would be something that would make you notice. Opening a barn door for the sheep standing out in a cold rain, or throwing a few grains of corn to the chickens are small things, but these little things begin to add up in you, and you can begin to understand that you're important. You may not be real important like people who do great things that you read about in the newspaper, but you begin to feel that you're important to all the life around you.

Nobody else knows or cares too much about what you do, but if you get a good feeling inside about what you do, then it doesn't matter if nobody else knows. I do think about myself a lot when I'm alone way back on the place bringing in the cows or sitting on a mowing machine all day. But when I start thinking about how our animals and crops and fields and woods and gardens sort of all fit together, then I get that good feeling inside and don't worry much about what will happen to me.

—Terry Cummins[7]

TRUTH SUDDENLY GRASPED

> "Ping" is the immediate recognition of a truth suddenly grasped and aptly conveyed—it is a quality writers work hard to achieve. Language carries both unconscious and conscious meaning. Writing can't ping until the two are integrated. When it finally "pings" we simply bow.
>
> —Gail Sher[8]

My computer helps me with my writing work. It has enormous capabilities, but I often feel a weary guilt for not working the programs and knowing the software better. Most of its power lies untapped beneath the niggling little messages it sends about improperly unplugging devices, and should it close this or that window since it has detected a black snake in the closet dressed in my grandmother's clothes. I was complaining about this to Rachel Baldwin, who relieved me of some false responsibility with: "Are you a little crazy? Would you rather be scraping hides and chewing sinew?" Those weren't her exact words, but there was a note of pure authority in her voice when she said, "No one uses even *close* to all the things their computer can do. There is *no reason* to. We each need our computers to perform a certain number of functions well, and other than that, it doesn't really matter what they are capable of doing in the hands of a geek."

Ping!! I simply bowed.

A YEAR OF REST FROM WORK

Reading about the Jubilee in *The Good Works Reader* and thinking of the poor of this world and those who suffer in both body and spirit right here in our own country: how we long for that year of liberation, that will take away everything that tears and breaks our lives and our land! This is what a very old patristic father named "Bede the Venerable" (672–735) had to say about the Jubilee:

> In the law, the fiftieth year was ordered to be called the year of jubilee, that is, "forgiving" or "changed." During it the people were to remain at rest from all work, the debts of all were to be canceled, slaves were to go free, and the year itself was to be more notable than other years because of its greater solemnities and divine praises. Therefore, by this number is rightly indicated that tranquility which provides the greatest peace. Then "the dead will rise and we shall be changed" (1 Cor. 15:52) into glory. Then, when the labors and hardships of this age come to an end, and

our debts, that is all our faults, have been forgiven, the entire people of the elect will rejoice eternal in the sole contemplation of the divine vision, and that most longed-for command of our Lord and Savior will be fulfilled: “Be still and know that I am God” (Ps. 46:10).

A DIARY OF LITTLE MATTERS

WINTER 2008

SMALL MATTERS

The ones "on which the daily happiness of private life depends."[1]

My niece Stephanie is only eighteen but so far in her short driving life, she has wrecked eight cars. (Not *all* were her fault.) This year her father, who has the patience of Saint Francis but is a lot funnier, beat us to the purchase of a new car. He'd never owned a new one either. His little red whatever-it-is, is just sweet, the way it handles, the way it looks. How I know is my sister let me drive it last summer.

I don't think it's an exaggeration to say Larry was hesitant to loan his spanking new car to his daughter. On the first occasion he let her drive, she returned with a deep scratch that ran from the front turn signal to the rear on the driver's side. Stephanie's honesty deserves admiration because she arrived home and went directly to her father. My brother-in-law wondered *what* she was doing or *where* she was looking to have not stopped even half-way through this etching. He was so dismayed he dismissed her from his presence with orders not to speak to him for a while. She waited three days, thinking she might even be willing to give up her cell phone for hurting his precious. When he finally allowed her back, he told her it was okay, a daughter was more important than a new car. I think that proves what I was saying about him. He's a saint.

I've been shrill about being far beyond the reach of American automakers and their ridiculous ads, but they found my idolatrous crack and now I must deal with a new flaw. I wonder if Jesus was really tempted in all ways like us—but without sin, of course—would he sit in the seat of a new car and savor the peculiar smell that tells you no one's owned this vehicle before? Would he be tempted to *love* the CD controls on the steering wheel? What I don't like about our old car is now unrestrained: humid weather makes it smell like dog's breath, and my shotgun seat looks like a moon crater. I want to be rid of the thing.

We are saving for a newer used car and yesterday we received a surprise gift from someone who loves us and worries about our safety when we drive long distances across the country in a car that has 180,000 miles on it. Her check fell out of the envelope and stunned us. The amazing gift came with the charge that we must add it to whatever we'd saved and buy a *new* car.

Denis has spent two days looking. I'm not going to a car lot unless there's a serious candidate. It's a pain in the . . . to spend so much time trying to make a decision and then negotiating with a salesperson who pretends he wants to know about your grandchildren. The cost of any low-end vehicle represents about half our annual income, so one option we *don't* need is a puddle light. Can you believe it? Eight hundred fifty extra dollars buys you floodlights so you don't step in a puddle on your way to the car in the dark. Is there some designer I can personally cudgel? On the other hand, I'm really interested in the seat warmer. Forget the twenty-seven airbags and the anti-lock brakes. On a cold day in Minnesota? I want the dial set on broil and my rear tenderly baked and supported any time the temperature is below fifty degrees.

Today we bought it—a 2007 pearl blue Ford Taurus. I like the color and it has the seat warmers. I'm trying not to, like, *love* it. That might be idolatry. Tonight I stare at the ceiling while lying in bed and imagine living in 1902 and taking the street car or walking everywhere I go. I'm sad we live in a time and place that requires commuting long distances for so many things, and sad for how much it costs. Even daily. But there is no way around this in our current times.

We've been parking Pearly Blue a few blocks farther from church on Sunday mornings because we're a little embarrassed about owning a brand new auto. It's been four weeks now and we finally received our license plates so at least the dealer plates which scream NEW CAR are gone and and a fine layer of dust dims the brand-new shine.

SLOW MATTERS

Amazing fact: A saguaro cactus does not put out its first arm—her signature reach to the heavens—until she is mature at fifty to one hundred years old.

I worked on *Quicken*[2] from 6:30–9:30 p.m. *Why* do I ignore bank statements for months at a time? Reconciling wouldn't take so long if I wasn't determined to not ask for help. I kept being five thousand dollars off. I *hate* stuff like this. Finally I broke down and called Denis. He had to be very, very careful because I'm dangerous like a black widow when angry. You see, sometimes he makes the mistake of asking questions that seem accusatory when he just wants information: *What have you done?!* He patiently looks at the figures and right *away* sees the problem.

It's been right in front of me the whole time. I want to become a Luddite. Go back to bartering. *Will you trade my cheese for your tomatoes?* Denis says, "Don't feel bad, it doesn't mean anything. For some reason I see numbers like you see colors."

I started crocheting again. *Save the Children* has a thing called "Caps to the Capital." All over the US, knitters and crocheters are making little hats for newborns. (Many emerging world babies have a low birth weight and chill easily, especially at night.) These will be added to national care packages sent to African countries. It seems so small, but it's what I can do. In spare moments I make them. There are now twenty tiny colorful little hats in a pile.

Denis and I have been arguing about scheduling details. I'm weary of it. We're so different, yet we're bound together by vows. We try starting anew and fail. Then I thought of repairing us with intimacy. While he sat in the bedroom reading, I prepared. But when I came back, he had gone downstairs to watch TV. I felt silly and forlorn. I pitched him a softball but he didn't know it was coming. When he came to bed I said, "Don't speak to me."

It takes a long time to grow that arm that reaches to the heavens. I wish maturity arrived faster. I am heartened by prayer and confession. At communion, when I eat the bread, I imagine every cell of my being becoming a part of Jesus. James Houston gladdens my heart. He's been a spiritual director for years and advises that it takes a long time to become the mature, godly person you assumed you would grow into overnight. He writes:

> I need a greater unity and integrity of faith, while realizing that any progress God gives occurs at the slowest pace of all!
>
> ...[W]e find that becoming Christlike progresses almost imperceptibly. For authentic integration we need to expect appropriate rates of apprehension, conversion, and transformation. Like the psalmist, we will experience orientation, disorientation, and reorientation as our emotions and desires are redirected and re-educated. Therefore we must maintain humility, gentleness, perseverance, fortitude, courage, and especially patience with ourselves as we pursue the journey.[3]

LITTLE PEOPLE MATTER

Drove North to Jerem and Micah's. Nearly nine hours in Pearly Blue. Looking forward to five days in charge of two little people while their parents are gone. Anson, three. Paige, one-and-a-half. Our grandchildren.

Day One. After two hours of snacks, fights, shooting of guns, and Bob the Builder screaming *CAN WE FIX IT? YES, WE CAN*, we walk to the post office. Took thirty minutes to dress them in snow pants, boots, hats, coats. I never could get their little balled up fists into their mitten thumbs. Thank God for Velcro. Just tighten the wrists and hope you haven't permanently cut off circulation. They plod along the cold, snowy street. Both of them purposefully fall straight down like an axed tree. They're so padded they bounce. Anson begins to lick snow off the street. There's about a half inch of new powder. He gets up, walks another fifty feet, does it again. Paige-y tries to copy him. I worry about poisons and pollutants. Finally give up telling him to stop, because he won't. The town is hushed. The streets are empty. A single dog has left tracks in the snow. Paige-y turns her sweet face to me, raises her arms, "Hode you, hode you?" she asks. "Yes, I'll hold you." I carry her the rest of the way. By the time we get to the post office Anson's face is dirty and wet. Snot is freezing on both their noses. A grizzled old guy pulls up to the curb in a rusty pick-up, jumps out, and holds the door open for us. "Yuh. Cold out ter today. Gettin' bad weather. Snow turning ta sleet. So then. Yup. I'll be seein' ya then."

Happy Paige on the "Whee."

They're napping now. So am I. The house is an astonishing wreck. How do young mothers do it? How did I?

Day Two. 6:00 p.m. I call my sister-in-law. "Is 6:30 too early to put them to bed?" We laugh. "No," she says.

Day Three. Unseasonable rain has coated everything in an armor of ice. There's a womens' Bible study at my sister's. With a babysitter! Hallelujah. It's only seventeen miles away and we're going. So what if it's ten degrees and the doors on Micah's van are frozen shut? We creep along on treacherous sheets of ice. I take a wrong turn. I cross the railroad tracks three times praying I don't stall in front of a Canadian Pacific and kill my grandchildren. The heater is barely working, but Paige-y is in her car seat stripping. She has her mittens and hat off and both feet are bare. Anson is reporting.

Day Four. Every day Denis has taken his work into town to a cute little coffee café with free wireless, espresso, and all that. A tiny familiar resentment from long ago creeps in. The morning was okay until about 10:30 when everyone got hungry and crabby. They like to walk up behind each other and give a whack on the back of the head just for the heck of it. Elemental proof of the need for redemption. The next moment Anson hugs Paige-y and plants a kiss on her mouth.

Couldn't find Paige-y's sippy cup anywhere. It's the only one she has and she wants it now. Searched and searched while she cried. Finally found it in the trash. It got there by itself, I suppose.

Day Five. Denis home by noon. I said he must be back by then. He walked to the post office with Anson. Six inches of new snow. It poofs with each step. Anson is so happy to be outside. Paige-y howls at the window, heartbroken at being left behind. I can't bear her disappointment so I dress her in snow gear. In the yard she plays on the "Whee." I help her climb up and she slides down into the snowdrift about a million times.

After supper I sit dangerously close to them on the couch. They're throwing themselves down on the cushions which to them is hilarious entertainment. The air around Paige-y grows acrid—her diaper hangs low and heavy, every gel capsule filled to capacity. How long had I forgotten to change her?

I ask, "Is your diaper soppy?"

"Yuh." Her stock answer to every question.

"Is your diaper poopy?"

"Yuh."

"Have you been eating rotting deer carcass again?"

"Yuh."

My vocabulary has pretty much been reduced to *hode-you, poopy,* and demands for *joose!* Life's little essentials.

Home. I miss them. Their dear little voices raised in woe. Their tired heads on my shoulder. We understand the value of suffering, but would still spare them from all the grief and tragedy they will face in life. If we could.

RENEWAL MATTERS

Driving home from St. Louis after speaking at a conference. A comfy, quiet ride in the new Pearly Blue. Talking about our future. Our vows. For richer, for poorer. In sickness, in health. I say to Denis, quoting Bob Dylan: "Stick with me, Baby. I'm sticking with you. Life is goin' to get interestin' right about now."

Last night we climbed into bed in the soft lamp light. I folded down the top of our white cotton blanket. His side is yellowed and limpy feeling again. What's with the male body?[4] He disavows. Says I merely turned the blanket to *look* like it's coming from his side.

Is 6:30 too early for bed?

Denis isn't feeling well. He has a cold, maybe a sinus infection. Last night as he fell into bed he moaned, "I'm just going to lie here and make my blanket yellow."

Today he leaned on the doorway of the guest bedroom, watching me pull old clothes from the closet and dump them on the floor. I was in a cleansing mood. He'd come down the hall from his office to investigate when he heard several blasts on a trombone and smelled gun smoke. I'd found Jerem's old instrument and a cute little cap gun which popped off when I pulled the trigger.

Denis said the nicest thing. He loves me because I'm whacked out and surprise him. I had no idea. I was only amusing myself. I was thinking of getting rid of the cap gun and the trombone, but perhaps I should save them.

I stopped rummaging and lay down on the bed, and he sat on it, leaning against the wall, closed his eyes and talked. About us, family, the church, where or if we should move and then he said, "I don't want to live."

Only in the past year have I understood that feeling. It's not aggressively self-destructive. It's a kind of tiredness. Sometimes you want to lie down and not get up again for a while because you've lost the heart and energy to walk.

I think a lot of it is lack of margin. Emotionally, spiritually, physically—he needs to be restored. I know he'll feel better, renewed, if he has some time to recover.

Day off. A warm spring day. We packed books and a lunch, bought *The New York Times* and headed to Wabasha on the Mississippi River. We drove the new car blasting Neko Case. We didn't even read much. Just sat. Stared at the water, watched boats sail in and out of the marina. Their first launch coming out of storage after a long winter. About the middle of the afternoon Denis said, "I haven't felt this happy in a long, long time."

Later. Denis thought about life without me. From our bed we watched a wind storm bend the trees. He said if I were to die first he would fade away. I think he'd get involved in his work and writing. I agreed: there's a lot we do without connecting consciously to the reasons that give them meaning. I make the bed, prepare a meal, pay the bills partly because I live with someone I love. When he was in Africa for two weeks, we were completely out of touch. I savored the first three days of freedom. Then I no longer made the bed. Decisions about food became boring. I stood in front of the refrigerator, ate carrot sticks, and drank juice from the carton. Evenings stretched long and silent and I kept the phone beside me, just in case, but it hardly rang. Then I wondered how it would feel to be widowed or to have always been single. Easy to ignore those who are.

This morning it's raining gently. Dim inside. Cold out. The birds come to the feeder outside my office window. Bedraggled, hungry, they cling upside down on the suet and swing on the feeder to grab a sunflower seed. Dear little wisps of God's creation. Chickadees, nuthatches, downy woodpeckers waiting for earth's complete redemption. *Palingenesia.*

ULTIMATE MATTERS

Lake Superior, North Shore. So quiet here. So lovely. Have been waiting months for this. The horizon is empty from edge to edge. Nothing but the lake surface moves, gently breathing in swells as far as the eye can see. The sky is gray. Water, rocks, trees, all are gray. Mesmerizing. My mind slowly empties and my heart drains its cares away. This must be the Wayside Inn from *Pilgrim's Progress.* Staying forever would be nice, but we're just here to refit.

Home. Staying in bed this morning. Drinking the tea Denis brought. It's gray and drizzly outside, but I'm elated. Last night I beat a bladder infection by slamming sixteen ounces of unsweetened cranberry juice *four* times. You can't imagine how macho I feel—proud to skip urgent care.

Minutes later, doubled in pain, high fever, on way to doctor with what is now a kidney infection. I beat nothing! Feel totally miserable. The doctor is kind and doesn't mention how inadvisable to self-medicate certain things.

Celebrating! Much better today. Fantastic how one moment you don't want to live and the next you're hungry and making cornmeal pancakes with real maple syrup.

I only know one Greek word—*dolmades* (stuffed grape leaves, they're yummy). But I just learned another. Transliterated, it is *palingenesia*. The phonetic spelling is pal-ing-ghen-es-ee'-ah. It rhymes with "I have raging diarrhea." Never mind how it sounds, you should love what it means. It is *all* the following: new birth, reproduction, renewal, re-creation, regeneration. The New Testament Greek dictionary gives several uses of the word. My favorite:

> ...the signal and glorious change of all things (in heaven and earth) for the better. That restoration of the primal and perfect condition of things which existed before the fall of our first parents.

It's only found twice in the New Testament.

> Jesus said to them, "Truly I tell you, at the renewal (*palingenesia*) of all things, when the Son of Man sits on his glorious throne..." (Matthew 19:28).

> But when the kindness and love of God our Savior appeared, he saved us, not because of righteous things we had done, but because of his mercy. He saved us through the washing of rebirth and renewal (*palingenesia*) by the Holy Spirit... (Titus 3:4–5).

This deep and glorious healing of all things through Christ is so certain, Paul speaks of it as if it had already happened. It's what is referred to as *now, but not yet*. When everything around invites us to despair, *palingenesia* keeps us crocheting little hats, changing diapers, writing against deadlines, deciding to live again. Rescue and regeneration: it's that perfect Garden we've longed for ever since we had to leave. It will be, *already is*—ours.

SKIRTING THE FLEECE

WINTER 2011

> Come now, let us reason together... though your sins are like scarlet, they shall be as white as snow; though they are red as crimson, they shall be like wool. (Isaiah 1:18)

I love these words because they tell us some interesting things about God. In the first phrase, he invites us to consider a pretty uncomfortable topic. God says, "Let's talk about your conduct, your life, and a few other matters. Take any standard of morality—even the low bar you set up yourself, and let's say nothing about the Ten Commandments—and then tell me how that's working for you. Can you have this conversation or are you afraid I can't forgive what you've done and love you at the same time? Give me your best shot."

God's desire to communicate on such a personal level is staggering. The invitation is brilliant. It deconstructs my prickly defense and causes me to listen.

White as snow, I understand. We have a lot of it right now; you probably do, too. All I need to do is look out the window. But to sharpen the analogy, in case we don't understand snow, God mentions wool for us to consider: "Though your sins are red as crimson, they shall be like wool." Did you know crimson and scarlet are colorfast dyes? You can't change your mind once they get into a fiber. They are indelible. When wool is first sheared from a sheep, it's not a brilliant shade of white or even cream, so I needed help enriching this analogy.

If we lived in an agrarian culture and raised sheep, we might understand it better. We might *know* what skirting a fleece means. I didn't until two years ago, when Anita became our housemate, friend, and Ransom's Resident Assistant.

Some of the delight of having her around is I never know what's next—like right now in Mole's End, her living quarters, there are twenty-seven ugly, creepy worms gorging on mulberry leaf mash. These waxy creatures each have a small dark cord pulsing down the center of their backs: more creepy.

They are silk worms, about to spin the cocoons that make one of the earth's most exquisite fibers.

Last spring when she hauled in several giant gunny sacks of sheep fleece purchased from a flock owner and began prepping them for spinning by dumping them onto a large tarp in the backyard, I wondered how she'd ever get wool mittens and sweaters out of that filth. The first thing she had to do was skirt the fleece.

Raw fleece stinks and is dirty, with bits of straw and dung stuck to it here and there. The color is often an unpleasant shade of stained yellow. Skirting, the first step in cleaning, is to remove the organic matter and snip away the worst of the stains. I had no idea this work was part of what makes that creamy-white sheepskin tossed on the seat of my rocking chair so attractive and comfortable on a cold day.

It was after Anita skirted the fleece, then washed it in soapy water, rinsed it, and put it out to dry in the sun that the transformation became so apparent. Its beauty shone. It smelled natural and fresh and the color was almost pure white.

God uses a metaphor right out of the shepherd culture where Isaiah lived. He links the erasure and forgiveness of our all our wrongdoing to a filthy fleece that has been turned into soft, pure-white wool. This transformation is what God means when he says your sins "shall be as wool."

Being married to one person for forty-three years is a part of my life's story. Wouldn't you think that after that long Denis and I wouldn't have much skirting to do? That we'd pretty much be white as wool? Well, no.

Last November we were on vacation. The quietness and beauty of the North Shore invites heart repair, renewal, and re-creation.

On the first day I did nothing unless absolutely necessary. Like shower. Did not make the bed or wash a single dish. Denis did that. I read. Stared out the window at the rocky shore and the gray sky. Went for a walk. Saw a big buck lying in the woods a few yards from the door, his antlers framed by bracken and tall grass. A bald eagle flew past the window. I didn't cook. Supper menu: half a smoked whitefish; rice crackers; carrot sticks. There was no hurry in anything we did.

On the second through fourth day, even though we were on vacation, we needed to do marriage care. Busyness, distance, offensive tones of voice, thoughtless reactions had built up. Like skirting a fleece, Denis and I needed to pick off the weeds stuck to our skin, the pieces of dung, the yellowed bits of marriage in need of washing. Sorry if you thought otherwise. Reconnecting in love and attachment isn't like eating vanilla pudding—a swish of the tongue and wow, you've eaten a quart. Sometimes it takes all our effort to remain attached and in love. It's work we don't really want to do—we'd rather be getting on with the fun stuff of vacation. On the other hand, forty-three years has taught us it

Anita skirts a fleece.

must be part of life. We're grateful that being where we are makes it possible to sit down beside one another with pen and paper, the book we're reading, a glass of wine, and talk. God is in the midst of us with his invitation and promise: "Come now and let us reason together."

A therapist friend recommended a book: *Hold Me Tight* by Sue Johnson. (I like to think the title, which I don't exactly appreciate, is the fault of the publisher's marketing department.) Johnson, a clinical psychologist, developed something called Emotionally Focused Couple Therapy (EFCT). It has a simple message: forget about learning how to argue better, analyze your early childhood, make grand romantic gestures, or experiment with new sexual positions. Instead, get to the emotional underpinnings of your relationship by recognizing that you are emotionally attached to and dependent on your partner in much the same way a child is dependent on a parent for nurturing, soothing, and protection. In this book, she teaches EFCT through a series of conversations and practical exercises to help couples create more secure and lasting bonds.

I'm pleased that her ideas helped us find ways to express what was troubling us and move us a little closer toward understanding and change. All of us hunger for safe emotional connections; we are hardwired to need this. It's in our blood. Our DNA. It's part of the inherited image of God planted within us. We long for it even more than food or sex. (Don't argue with me about this.) In marriage, Johnson writes, "Distressed partners may use different words but they are always asking the same basic questions. 'Are you there for me? Do I matter to you? Will you come when I need you, when I call?'"[1]

These questions are almost exactly the ones Denis and I have used to describe this generation's hunger for love and commitment in relationships. We've observed that the answer to these questions in so many instances is "No," accompanied by silence or abandonment by parents, lovers, friends, employers. In other words, no one will be there for you. I instantly recognize something of this in myself; the questions describe what I want from marriage. Denis does, too. We both want the answer to be: "Always."

As Denis and I read the book together, listened (that's hard work) to one another, and examined what the author calls "Demon Dialogues," we saw our own ways of going round and round a raw spot, arguing about exactly who said or did what. We want the other person to acknowledge our point and agree, but it ends up looking like the only way out is to admit you're the rotten spouse every single time. We end up with me angry and hostile, him withdrawn and cold.

We couldn't have scripted the spontaneous exchange we had that afternoon. Even as it happened, we knew it was a stupid-funny thing to quibble about. But it captured the essence of deeper struggles:

> D: What time is it?
>
> Me (I pick up my cell phone and look at the analog clock on the front): "5:30. Er, no. 6:30? Hmmm." (I look again because the hands are close.)
>
> D (Whips out his cell showing the time in digits): "5:34. This is better.
>
> (The instant he said that, I knew a look of hostility crossed my face and he saw it. In that second we understood where this was going and we chose to keep talking, and even laughing at the absurdity of it.)
>
> Me: "You've made a value judgment: your way is better. Therefore, my choice of analog is: Not better. Mine is Less better. It's not the right way. I'm wrong, therefore, I'm stupid—in your mind. But I'M NOT STUPID."
>
> D: "No! That's not what I meant. It has nothing to do with value judgment. There may be a ton of reasons why you'd have the other. In fact, one might be that it's more aesthetically pleasing. So saying 'This is better' wasn't meant to be a personal dismissal or condemnation of what you've chosen."

> Me: "But c'mon, when you say something is better, what do you mean by using that word? I have lots of trouble getting away from the feeling that I've just been, yeah, in a small way, but, still, I've been judged. Words mean something."
>
> D: "It's not like that at all. In fact"—I notice how he says "in fact" but talks about emotion. It's kinda endearing—"it hurts me that you immediately assume the worst. It's fine to have something different. I only meant that when you glance at it, digital is easier to read."

We agree I like spontaneity and freedom, and Denis likes clarity and precision more than I do. Control is important to him. He's hurt because he wants me to trust that he doesn't think I'm stupid.

I'm hurt because he said, "This is better." If I can be "right" about things, then it proves I've made a good choice and maybe he will love me more. Oy vey.

Both of us gained insight to help our relationship. I need to calm down and not be so quick to assume he's purposely being insensitive. He needs to think more carefully about his word choices. Beneath all this, what we both want is to be the other's love above all others.

A friend muses how funny-odd it is that sometimes seeing your spouse through another's eyes causes renewed appreciation. We watch them kindly pick up a child and offer a drink, or hear them patiently explain how to recover a lost file, or deliver a really fine lecture, and we are touched that the person is our friend and lover.

I know a book is not going to be the answer to every problem nor is Johnson's EFCT, though it has been helpful. Through the years, Denis and I have searched for a place of beauty for our love and commitment. We long to be bright, beautiful wool ready to be spun into all manner of artful coverings in service to one another and to Christ. Part of this service is truth-telling. To one another, and to you. Years of Christian practice do not guarantee a marriage that never needs skirting. Rather, here, in the midst of dust and wounds, we meet Christ and hope in his promise to make all things clean again.

I know we'll never be perfect, but we're growing. I see my spouse with refreshed eyes. The habits that annoyed me yesterday are strangely tolerable again, maybe even a little charming. I send Denis a quote from a comedian who says, "I love being married. It's so great to find that one special person you want to annoy for the rest of your life." We laugh.

THE NUTMEG OF CONSOLATION

WINTER 2011

I recently read about a man who was sent to Indonesia with his family to live and work for a global corporation. He had a lively interest in natural history, so in addition to his regular employment, he began describing, drawing, and writing about the island's plants. Having learned much about the flora from local people, he included extensive cultural lore and medicinal uses. He pressured himself to complete the drawings because he was losing his eyesight to glaucoma. The effort became a large body of work, so large he hoped to get it published.

Then came a series of tragic events. His wife and daughter were killed in a tsunami. Shortly after this, his house burned down and all his drawings were lost in the fire. He eventually had them redrawn with the help of an assistant. He sent half of the manuscript back to Europe, but the ship carrying it sank. Finally, after thirty-seven years of research, writing and rewriting, the completed manuscript reached his company's headquarters. However, the company decided to suppress publication, declaring that the manuscript contained trade secrets having to do with medicines and spices.

The year it arrived in Europe was 1697. His employer was the Dutch East India Company. The author, Georgius Everhardus Rumphius, died in 1702 without seeing his work published. It was finally printed in 1741, thirty-nine years after his death.

This seven-volume masterpiece, *The Ambonese Herbal*[1], was not available in English until Dutch scholar E.M. Beekman began the enormous process of translating it in the year 2000. That same year he was diagnosed with multiple myeloma. He, too, pushed himself to complete this massive project. It was finished in November of 2008, just before he died. This past year (2011), it was published posthumously by Yale Press. Beekman never saw his translation in print. I wish I could have consoled both of these men, assuring them that in a few years their work would be noted and loved by many. They bring us knowledge, yes, but they also bring us the pleasure of knowing God's astonishing, elaborate works of plant art on a tropical island.

Thus far, my life's work and calling have not taken such a beating, though I sometimes wonder about the meaning and worth of what I do. Or have done. I often feel small and insignificant. Perhaps I should have gone to law school or herded sheep, I think. Sometimes I complain that all I do is grind coffee beans and update my status on Instagram.

I have a book that was not shipwrecked, but for years it went unpublished. I think of the hours, months, even years it took to write. The days of crabbiness and distraction my husband endured as I wrote. The many drafts, the queries, and the rejections, and there it sits, its pages printed and bound on my shelf. I often wonder, "What is this other than a colossal waste of time and white paper?" And then, unlike Rumphius or Beekman, I lived to see *The Exact Place: A Memoir* finally published in 2012.[2]

I'm not alone in desiring consolation and comfort for merely keeping on year after year. I've had conversations with many folks from all walks of life who have had vocational questions about meaning and worth.

A dear friend who works in the top layer of a Fortune 500 company, has been a faithful employee, a consummate leader, and team player for many years. Recently, she attended an event where a few were recognized for their good work and asked to tell their stories. She knew one of these rising stars well because she had trained him. As he spoke, she was at once happy for him and a little sad. I think we understand why. It wasn't her need for power or fame; it was the desire to be acknowledged, to know her work has meant something. The speaker ended his talk by saying, "I wouldn't be up here today without the help of a person who has made my success possible. She has been my mentor and model—someone who encouraged me when things were hard, but who was tough enough to make me grow a spine. I would like to thank her." Then, he said her name. It was as though God himself heard her heart and suddenly named her in front of everyone.

Long ago in the same part of the world where Rumphius did his work, certain East Indonesian sultans were oddly referred to as "The Nutmeg of Consolation." This may have been related to the value of nutmeg, which was once worth its weight in gold, and also thought to be a cure for the plague. It's an intriguing title. It has a spicy, comforting sound that makes you think of holding a pottery mug with both hands and lifting it to your lips—a soothing mix of apple sweetness, wine and spice.

With a powerful sultan, if you were lucky, you might find both the pleasure of his rare presence and a remedy for your troubles. You might be comforted,

Thirty-six rejection slips for my first book, *The Exact Place.*

as his name implied. Might. If his curry agreed with him and his harem was in order. Of course, these rulers are dead now and their power is gone.

A similar title has attracted my attention and deep gratefulness many times. It appears in the Christmas story as told by Luke. It isn't noted often, yet the words stand out to me as comfort to a soul who considers them.

Two thousand years ago, when Jesus was eight days old, he was brought to the temple for dedication and circumcision. Joseph and Mary weren't expecting a special welcome from the establishment, but for years an old, old guy had been watching for this very person, and he spotted him in the crowd. A young couple was carrying him, a baby boy just over a week old.

Simeon, we are told, was "waiting for the Consolation of Israel" (Luke 2:25). How long had he been watching and waiting for this person? How did he recognize this particular baby? Did the hair stand up on the back of his neck? The Holy Spirit must have blazed inside him, because hurrying over and taking God in his arms, he cried, "My eyes have seen your salvation, which you have prepared in the sight of all people, a light for revelation to the Gentiles and for glory to your people Israel."

"The Consolation of Israel." An unusual title for a baby.

John Calvin once wrote in a letter to a prisoner held in a French dungeon, who was subsequently martyred, "We have wherewith to comfort ourselves in all our miseries, looking for that happy issue which is promised to us, that He will not only deliver us by His angels, but will Himself wipe away the tears from our eyes."[3]

Jesus is the only one with everlasting presence and the divine power to console us from our sin. To comfort us in darkness. To allay the sorrow and the weariness of everyday life. To grant us worth and meaning, not only in our vocation and calling, but for our very selves.

Over and over, it is our privilege to offer up to Jesus the small, everyday works from our hands. It is the labor of my listening and writing. It is the apple puff pancakes I made this morning for houseguests. It is loving ten Angora baby bunnies, tiny creatures of God, who dart to my feet expecting kale and carrots each morning as I step onto the back porch where they will live until our housemate sells them. Jesus is our comfort and consolation for things unfinished, for futures unknown. He is the keeper of life's collateral results hidden from our eyes.

The Consolation of Israel arrived with an express purpose: to one day restore glory to everything that has gone awry. Peter refers to this in the book of Acts when he speaks of Jesus coming again (Acts 3:21). This is part of the joy and comfort we share with Simeon as we wait for Jesus to finish what he has already begun.

A note about *The Nutmeg of Consolation.*

You might recognize this as the title of a book in Patrick O'Brian's series of seafaring novels set in the early 1800s. In O'Brian's book, it is both the name of a ship and a piece of music. In rare moments of peace, onboard the ship, Captain Aubrey and Stephen Maturin, the ship's surgeon, play duets on the violin and cello. On one such occasion Aubrey asks Maturin, "I dare say, what was that last piece?"

> Maturin's reply: "Nutmeg of Consolation." Aubrey thinks about this and says, "That's it. Those were the very words hanging there in the back of my mind. What a glorious name for a tight, sweet, newly-coppered broad-buttock little ship—a solace to any man's heart... Dear Nutmeg. What joy."[4]

Yes. To see the Nutmeg hove into sight, her sails sheeted to the wind, and you castaway on an island without hope of rescue? That, my friends, is Divine Consolation.

TOOTHPASTE IN THE TOILET

FALL 2012

"Dude!! you need to chill!"

I don't ordinarily talk like this, calling someone "Dude." It's pretentious for a woman my age. But it seemed appropriate at the time. I had to shout to get Denis' attention because he was flipping out.

He walked into the bedroom late one night and asked why there was water under the lid of the flip-top toothpaste container. When he opened it a bunch had spilled out. Well. I remember thinking for a second: *Margie, you need to lie here. Because you love him.* But I couldn't think fast enough. I told the truth.

"I dropped it in the toilet."

Before I could assure him that I had washed it with hot water and soap, he was yelling, so what could I do? I hadn't thought of opening the lid to drain it. He was acting like he was going to be infected with flesh-eating bacteria or something.

I *told* him there was nothing in the bowl, except water, and all you might get is a little pink eye, ha-ha. (In case you don't know—pink eye is caused by fecal contamination.) He didn't think that was funny. As he went down the hall, he was still shouting, "*What* were you thinking?" and et cetera.

A while later I got up to do something and saw he'd thrown away the toothpaste *and* his toothbrush. So I had to ask, "What were *you* thinking? Like we can afford to throw away a perfectly good container of toothpaste? *And* your toothbrush, too? What will all our ministry's donors think of being so wasteful? And after we told them how hard times were?"

I don't know whether I should report what he said, but it was: "And *every* time I *find* that toothpaste back on the shelf I *will* throw it away."

So touchy! I told him not to touch it any more. The next day I bought him a new container of Crest. (I'll use up the old one myself.) The problem is that the new one looks exactly like the old one, and in a few weeks (until he reads this) he'll forget. And with our memory problems, well, you can see where this might lead.

Unhappily, in my life there are other categories of lost and fallen. To me, flying is like entering another dimension; you leave the airport in Minneapolis and arrive at Hogwart's Castle with body and mind intact. But when we flew to our annual board meeting in January, I lost my socks in that magical dimension. As we settled into our narrow little seats, I got hot. After adjusting the air, removing several layers of clothing, and still feeling frantic, I took off my shoes and socks, leaving them on the floor beside my computer case.

When we were about to land and I was re-dressing, I couldn't find my socks. Although we looked everywhere, they were gone. I decided not to worry because we landed in Phoenix where, what the hey, it's warm and my socks had holes in them anyway. But, still, I wonder, is it me? The universe? Or what?

Then there is my key ring with front door, back door, storm door, and car keys that I cannot find. Unlike my cell phone which can be called from our landline to discover its location, I can't call my keys. I hoped they were just bouncing around in my purse, but apparently not. So, I retraced a week's worth of errands, begging clerks and cashiers to check the lost and found. This happened while Denis was out of town with our car and I was borrowing Anita's second set of keys to drive her car. I thought about praying to find my keys until Denis showed me a *New Yorker* cartoon where an angel appears at the window of an overweight, disheveled-looking man, kneeling beside his bed and announces, "Your prayers are freaking God out." I'm freaking myself out.

It may be risky to reveal more about who I am, but what do I have to lose? I have a more serious problem with breaking the Tenth Commandment. Thou shalt not covet.

In an excellent book on his search for humility, Bruce Ray Smith writes:

> I admit to envy, a sin I deprecate in others and to which I had thought myself immune. Envy is a strain, a virulent strain, of pride: I should not be so surprised, so mortified to find myself infected.[1]

So yes, I admit my envies include the following:

First envy: A writing retreat house. A sweet little cabin (designed by architect Andrew Berman) caught my attention because it was posted online. It is aesthetically gorgeous with calm colors and tidy shelves. A wide, clean desk faces a wall-sized window overlooking a sunny woods. Right now the ceiling of the office where I write is leaking. I was out running errands when my husband heard a rhythmic plop, plop, plop-plop and investigated. Water was dripping onto my bookshelves, open dictionary, and a stack of papers. The ceiling is now drooping and stained the color of tobacco juice. Then I recalled a writer who wrote every day from a tiny desk jammed into her small, dark closet that smelled like an old shoe.

I have a window that looks out on a luxurious linden tree. I have a small tapestry that softens the wall above my desk. The floor is honeyed-colored fir, and my messy L-shaped desk is large enough to host a sweet collection of giraffes. The bathroom is right next door. Bonus!

Second envy: A successful nonprofit organization. I admired the way this organization celebrated their twentieth anniversary this past year. When I heard that a couple of crack chefs were coming from far away to help cook a feast for the attendees, I blushed. What? Why didn't Ransom do something like that for our twentieth anniversary? Back then, Denis thought of splurging on a roll of foil stickers we could place on envelopes announcing: Celebrating 20 Years! But wait, wasn't this our own failure of imagination? We had no energy or ambition to do more. Should friends be faulted for doing what they do so well—mentoring and launching gifted musicians and artists? Ransom's thirtieth anniversary is coming up next year. So. Margie? Never mind, I get where this is going.

Third envy: Friends who took a trip to France. This couple sent secret waves of envy through my heart. During grape harvest? Fromage fests? Café crème on the plaza? They are precious friends who have hosted us many times and spent countless hours loving us through dark and fainting times. And last November, didn't I get not only what I needed, but just what I wanted, after all? A quiet place on a lake without television or neighbors? A fireplace, windows to the sun, books, coffee and a good companion? Yes, I did.

I'd like you to think I'm better than this. Kinder, more generous. But even that is a desire fueled by pride. What God has in mind is something radical and painful, a deeper magic—the stripping of my walls down to the studs. He wants to remake me.

Again, Smith's honesty helps me admit who I am:

> I want to be cured of the ills with which my pride afflicts me. But even without them, even freed from isolation, contempt and self-contempt, I will be no better. I still won't know how to live; I won't know, not here nor in heaven, how to be until I learn who I am, who I am now and who God meant, means, me to be.[2]

So, me too. I want to be who God intends me to be. To trust that his plan to restore all things doesn't only include freedom from the stress of lost keys or toothpaste dropped in the toilet. Way more importantly, I will be restored and will never envy ever again.

SAY "I LOVE YOU"

WINTER 2012

When I grew up and moved away I rarely saw them. But in December of every year I especially remember my grandparents. Each December I carefully add a small collection of bubble lights to the tree, placing them just so because, I admit, too many would be slightly cheesy. Their gentle movement and glow add a dimension to our Christmas tree that I must have. It's the memory of my grandparents' tree in full regalia.

Grandpa and Grandma Frolander made Christmas special for our family of eight. And, just as importantly, they never forgot my birthday, which was December 15th—a birth date easily rolled into Christmas. Some years on Christmas Eve they drove drifted country roads far out to our small farmhouse, bringing two (two!) presents for every child. Grandma also brought tins filled with cookies. Tender thumbprint cookies with a dollop of apricot jam in the center, fragile Swedish rosettes dusted with powdered sugar, and pressed butter cookies in the shape of bells decorated with tiny silver balls. Everything she did was precise and beautiful.

Sometimes I went home with them and in the morning when I awoke in a chilly bedroom alone, I would creep down the stairs and climb into my grandparents' bed. Grandma would already be up making breakfast—the coffee pot wheezing in the kitchen, the air filled with the scent of bacon. Grandpa would be in bed still listening to NBC News on the radio. I would snuggle under the blankets and he would reach over, just as I knew he would, and pinch me. I would scream. He would tickle me. I would hit and kick him. He would grab my fingers and not let go, no matter how I screamed and laughed, until Grandma came in saying, "Oh, for heaven's sake, Pete. Stop making that child scream." It was a good way to begin Christmas vacation.

Me and Grandpa Frolander, a man I loved.

Over the years we wrote to one another and twice they visited us in New Mexico. The last time Grandma remembered my birthday was December 1980. A few days after she mailed the card, they both died. Grandpa had finished lunch that day and moved to his living room chair where he was finishing the wooden clocks he was making for his grandchildren. They were gathered around his feet, ready for clockworks and hands. After Grandma washed the lunch dishes, she went into the living room to knit and found him sitting unnaturally still, his head fallen forward. She called my mother, who lived thirty-six miles away, to say, "Dad has just died."

Mom told Grandma to hang on, and she would be there as fast as ever she could. When she arrived in Warroad, she saw the ambulance in their driveway, and a crew carrying a body out of the house on a stretcher. She assumed it was her dad and did not, could not, comprehend the shocking words: "No, this is your mother."

She had gone, too.

As the family gathered from faraway places, Mom and her brothers met at their house to plan, to be together. I listened to their talk and tried to grasp, tried to believe that both Grandpa and Grandma were gone. The house was decorated. Sitting at the kitchen table, drinking Grandma's coffee and seeing plates of Grandma's Christmas cookies, divinity, and fudge on the counter, I remembered the loveliness of her hands as she baked and carefully decorated dozens of goodies. Now, this surreal moment as we sat nibbling her sweets. How could she not be here?

I regretted I hadn't thanked them enough for their gifts, for their love. So my advice is: say it. If your grandparents are living, say "I love you." Say it now. I only wish that I had taken more time to write and call. I believe I will see Grandma again, and will be able to tell her how much I love her. We aren't as certain of Grandpa, but there is evidence that in his final days he may have called out to God.

Someone pointed out I may be overemphasizing how the way Home to God is through recognizing his love for us. We simply reach out for him. Myself, I responded to God's love from the time I was a child and found him to be there for me. It seems to be a theme that appears and reappears in the way I talk, the way I write. That friend's observation pushed me. Just because that was my experience of coming to Christ, that doesn't mean everyone has the same one. To the extent I imply this is the norm, I wish to correct that impression.

Author Ellis Potter reminds us:

> We are each different. I can tell you how and why I came to be a Christian, but you cannot do it that way. You have to do it your own way. You are not me. You are unique. You have to come to God and God has to come to you in a way that you understand intellectually, emotionally, existentially, and morally, in ways that I might not understand. According to the Bible, your relationship to God is like a marriage. Christians often speak of sharing their faith, but I don't believe I can share my faith. I think I can share the faith—what is believed by Christians—but I cannot share my faith any more than I can share my marriage. I have a marriage, and I can tell you about it, but I cannot share it with you. I have a faith in Jesus Christ, and I can tell you about it, but I cannot share it with you. You have to have your own. You cannot have it by copying another person, or by inheriting it from your parents or your grandparents. We can say that God has no grandchildren. He only has children. Each one has to come directly to him.[1]

I believe he is right. Easily, easily, off the top of my head I can tell you about three people who came to Jesus in very different ways. My mother came to belief out of fear of going to hell and the fear that she would colossally fail her six children by not teaching them the gospel if it was true. What would she say to God when he asked her about her six children?

A friend, an undergraduate in college, was on his way to class one day when his bicycle got a flat tire. He was repairing it beside the curb when a member of a Christian campus organization walked past and trapped him into listening to a memorized presentation of the "Four Spiritual Laws." This person was extremely annoying and our friend was in no mood to hear him, but he couldn't get the "Laws" out of his head. Later that night, he turned to Christ.

One more example. Trevor, a young man we knew back in the day, came to our New Mexico commune because he had a vision of Jesus. He had been on an acid trip and Jesus spoke to him from the cross. He was deeply moved. Trevor knew nothing about Christianity, but he heard we were Christians and he wanted to become one. I'm not recommending this particular way, just saying…

I'm grateful for the differences, for the surprising ways people reach out to God and find, there he is, ready to meet us wherever we are, even with our doubts and unanswered questions. God operates unfathomably outside my box. I think this may be the core Gift of Christmas—that Christ was born to bring us an amazing salvation, and he has the power to bring us Home in a thousand ways from a thousand places in the wilderness. So I don't care how my grandfather came to God. If he did. I just want to meet him again when I die.

In *The Exact Place* I included a recipe from Grandma Frolander—Lemon Angel Pie. She made it for holiday meals, and it is so good that I included it again in this book. It was always a part of Christmas and it became one of my mother's traditions, too. We looked forward to this light-as-air dessert. There was always room for it even though we were stuffed with mashed potatoes, turkey, gravy, dressing, and cranberries. The lemon pie—intense filling, lightly sandwiched between two layers of whipped cream, resting on a crunchy meringue—is still one of my favorite desserts. A bite of heaven. Perhaps it will be featured at God's Table? I don't know.

But when I make it now, it is a pleasing bite—a taste, perhaps, of a more perfect life—one where we remember to say "I love you." On time. Where death no longer stalks us, because it's been conquered by our Friend and Savior, Jesus. So, forever and ever may Christmas always be merry to you.

THE MOUNTAIN ASH

SPRING 2013

This past summer we lost our mountain ash. For three years it has shown signs of sickness. The first year I was hopeful. It was just my imagination. It was a dry year. Leaves were withering and falling in midsummer. When I looked closely at the bark, in places it looked like it was giving up the trunk, loosening like a roll of paper towels ready to unravel.

The next year I noticed dozens of small, even holes drilled in such perfectly straight rows you'd have thought a tiny engineer with a miniature drill was at work, but it was woodpeckers going after wormy invaders. Normally, the tree produced clusters of bright red berries each fall, but last year they, too, were sickly looking. The crowds of cedar waxwings that visited once a winter to feast on them did not come. In hopes of stopping the spread, we cut off the worst-looking limbs. The continued yellowing of branches at the ends of main limbs sent me googling arborist sites. It had fire blight, an incurable bacterial infection. It was useless to fight it. Like pouring gasoline on coals.

Sadly, we cut it down. The cross section of the trunk showed dark streaks, evidence of the secret disease that ran up its vascular system, plugging its only way to get nutrition.

Mountain ash is a northern tree that likes cold winters. I planted this tree ten years ago in memory of my Frolander grandparents. Mountain ash thrived on the resort Grandpa and Grandma owned on a remote island on the Canadian side of Lake of the Woods, and at their winter home in the town of Warroad, Minnesota. Mountain ash don't need rich soil, they efficiently pull nutrients from rocky, cold earth. They often grow up clump-like, as birch do, sending up several strong leaders from the ground that eventually become trunks. Their branches bend in graceful arcs, especially in fall when berry clusters weigh them down. However, the farther south they roam, the more susceptible they are to fire blight. So Rochester is a trial for them.

This past fall, as we often do, we headed to the North Shore of Lake Superior where a friend owns a cabin about fifty feet from the water's edge. Here is where we've been fortunate enough to land for a restorative week now and then. The south-facing windows give a full view of cold, rocky shoreline and glorious sunrises and sunsets. One week here can make up for months of city living, bounded on all sides by neighbors and trees. All along Highway 61, we passed mountain ash glowing wildly, bent with scarlet berries. They shone among forests of yellow birch leaves, white trunks, and dark evergreens.

Mountain ash trees poignantly remind me of my Grandpa and Grandma who loved me well as a child. Now, it's odd to think that I am a grandparent, yet I still miss them. I've reached their time of life. We have eight grandchildren, and beyond wanting to love them well, we are becoming more familiar with the changes and limitations this age brings. Here we are, Denis and I, just passing sixty-five and entering this inevitable stage of life that everyone slides toward. We aren't ready to retire yet, but we are actively considering the changes knocking on our door.

The autoimmune issues I have can sap my energy and fog my brain. There are days when lifting the lid on my computer feels hard. I cancelled my October trip to Alaska for a women's retreat because at the time I didn't think I could manage it. More often now I hear Denis say, "Let's just have a quiet evening at home, please?" I can't do hospitality at the same pace or other things I have loved doing at Toad Hall when I did not give a single thought to the energy required. Not anymore. We couldn't have done the past five years without help from Anita, our assistant. I've wondered, apart from the physical challenges, why can't I accomplish more here? I think I know. God seems to be leading us in a little different direction. We've concluded we need to leave Toad Hall.

In an NPR interview, the music duo Over the Rhine recently talked about their latest CD and some other things that resonated deeply in my heart. Karin Bergquist said:

> We lived in the city for a long time and we loved it. It just became more and more obvious to us that we needed a change when we would get home from tour, traveling city to city; we started craving something else. And so, this last chapter, the last eight years of our lives, have been centered around [Nowhere Farm in Ohio]. It's about an hour outside of the city. I wanted coffee and birds and dogs and silence; I just needed that for a change …
>
> There's a line in there [from a song titled "Meet Me at the Edge of the World"] about how we're standing on this cold concrete, we're performing on this stage and we're so, so grateful for the

> audience that is here—but there's still that calling, that craving to be alone and to be someplace where we can sort of collect ourselves and plug in and rejuvenate and recover. That's where the songs come from, that moment of recovery.[1]

I don't think of my life as being on a stage where I perform as Over the Rhine has, but we do have a life filled with people and all sorts of urban events. For thirty-two years it has been something of a public life. Now it seems that rather than just taking off for a few weeks during the year, we are looking for a more permanent place where there is less noise and more quietness and rejuvenation that allows us to write not songs, but words.

All my life I have longed for a more rural setting, but heeding God's call has meant living in the city. So there, we created a place of shelter and discussion and hospitality and writing. We made a small, quiet garden in the midst of the foot traffic and buses, ambulances and helicopters that coursed by Toad Hall each day.

Our Mountain Ash tree in winter.

The farm I grew up on had its difficulties, but its long horizons and starry nights have never left me. They still call to me in a way I hardly recognized or owned as a younger woman. I've always said to Denis that when I'm old, all I want is a *Room with a View*. Remember that movie? Of course, I've amended that a little. Now I add: hardwood floors, a burr coffee grinder, and a comfy bed on the main level because some days I haul myself up the stairs like an old goat with a cane.

A country setting is not where we plan to do nothing, but a place where as long as our battered brains hold up, we will write and include some thoughtfully chosen travel gigs. Lots of folks have asked if there would be a next volume of *The Exact Place*.[2] It's somewhere in my head, but I need to get there fast as memories flee. My editor would like me to (kindly) get off my duff and pull together a collection of *Notes.*

My heart longs for the horizon—a place where my eyes rest somewhere beyond my desk, where I sit with my pad and pencil and a cup of coffee, looking at that distant place where the sun rises and sets. I'd like to see a field with wooly animals, fainting goats, and a little coop with five or six barred hens. I'm sure those creatures will help me remember who I am and what God made me for. Perhaps the refreshment I seek will turn into fruit that God might be pleased to use in my final run down to the end of the garden.

So this is, perhaps, the winter of our lives. Or at least late fall. There is still lots to be done. Denis wants to keep writing *Critique.* I'd like to keep on letting you know how this aging bit goes. Is it possible to serve God well with failing body parts, social security, and Medicare? We plan to lean into this and listen and learn new ways of being faithful in the midst of our ordinary. We'd like to be signposts of encouragement to others. We are going to avoid the advertisements of our culture that insist *You can do anything you want no matter how old you are.* Bah. Denis jokes that we're not quite ready for assisted care, but "perhaps we'll name our next home 'The Out House,'" since it'll be the last place we own, somewhere out there on the prairie, on our way out of life. And, bonus! He suggests I write "Sheets from the Out House."

Maybe. Maybe.

EVERY LITTLE THING

FALL 2013

Today I tripped and fell and it felt like a warning.

I left for the mall this morning after a meeting with Marcy, Ransom's bookkeeper. It had to be a quick stop on my way to the bank. After my business at the mall, I quickly headed for the car. Looking up and down the row, I could not see the car anywhere. What? I pressed the panic button on my keys but didn't hear a horn blaring. I stood puzzled. These are frightening moments for people my age. Our brains begin frantically beeping. Red alert! Red alert! And worse than the brain not finding a reasonable explanation is when it finds nothing at all.

I usually remember where I park by recalling the direction I was headed when I found an empty spot—was I pointed toward the entrance or away? Hmmm. I knew it was toward. Wasn't it? I looked in the next row, but the car wasn't there either. Or in the next row. Or the next.

About that time, a young woman getting out of her SUV stopped to ask if I'd lost my car. Was my wandering that obvious? Embarrassed, I admitted yes. She sympathetically recalled, "I did that just last week. Looked everywhere. Couldn't remember where I'd parked. What color is your car?" She was determined to help.

"Dark blue Ford 500."

"Why it's right there!" she exclaimed. "Oops, no, that's a Chevrolet. Shall I drive you around? I can do that. Why don't I?"

"No, no, it's okay, it's got to be right here somewhere." By then I was ready to call Denis to report our car had been stolen. "Really," the lady insisted, "I can take you." This was too much kindness; I had to refuse. I should be the one showing kindness to strangers, not receiving it. I am self-sufficient. I can fix anything.

She finally left me in a desert of cars and walked toward the doors. Complete in my humiliation, I looked up at the sky, and that was when, through some kind of electrifying nerve burst (God? Holy Spirit?), I remembered I had driven Anita's car, not our own. Her car happened to be the one right in front of me. I gave a loud groan (I may have cussed) and the lady who was still within earshot hollered, "Did you find it? Did you find it?!" Then, I had to explain I had forgotten I'd borrowed a car. This does not really explain, though, does it?

I headed to the bank in a greater hurry to get back home because I had important writing deadlines, and needed to be putting words to paper right that second. As I left the bank, I passed Marcy on her way in with a Ransom deposit. I waved and smiled.

Outside, I stopped and thought, *Why, Margie, you could save her a trip back to our house if you waited a minute for the receipts.* That was when I turned around to run back in, tripped on the curb and fell face down. I could say this was caused by the achy joints I'd been nursing all week, but again, I don't think that entirely explained what was happening either.

For what seemed like hours, I lay on the sidewalk. More humiliation. Why did God allow this? (God is remarkably patient with unjustified blame.) My knee felt exploded, my wrist hurt, and I had managed to hit my lip on the sidewalk. Our bank is a very quiet place and not a soul came in or out, nor did a car drive past as I finally pulled myself to a sitting position and sat thinking that if anyone did come along and express the smallest degree of sympathy I would begin sobbing. No. I'd wail. Loud, mournful howls. With more groaning, I hoisted myself up and hobbled to the car.

I'm home now. Working from bed. I was planning on having what I call a "Bed Day" anyway, because I need a little extra time for recovery from recent travels. Now that my fall has added more body parts to the problem, I wonder how to get everything done that needs doing. I've received plenty of sympathy here at home. Denis teases me, saying I should begin using a walker (right, dude), but he brought me iced tea, my cell phone, and a pillow. Anita says she'll make lunch. She made supper, too.

That morning, I had awakened early from a fitful night of not sleeping. Denis seemed awake when I asked him about a dilemma I was pondering: I need to finish writing the next issue of *Notes From Toad Hall* and it takes hours of concentrated writing. There is no way I'll make the deadline on Saturday.

The problem is we're planning to go away for two nights this weekend. Days off are difficult to manage at home because Toad Hall is also our work and where our offices are located. Work is everywhere and calls to us. From the basement to the attic, we hear it: emails, emails, emails. Phone calls. Doorbell, doorbell. Sometimes we go away to escape them.

I thought of three options for dealing with my deadline:

1. Simply look at the days as time off for Denis' sake, not mine, of course. I would go along, but keep working.
2. Limit self to three hours of work each day and let the remaining hours be time off the grid.
3. Just believe I need this time away, too. Kick my schedule in the rear. I made it up myself, after all, not some CEO who threatens my job.

With half his brain intact, Denis mumbled, "Number three," and fell back asleep.

I decided to stick with his call. But it's not easy. I am a responsible, committed, dependable, hardworking woman, and God forbid someone should find me floating on an air mattress in some lake somewhere.

I know, that's a little sick.

Maybe that's what the fall was about? I tripped and finally heard a message? You fall down, wreck your knee, hobble around with a walking stick, and are forced to go to bed immediately after supper, because you think you need to fix and save every little whatever?

God is speaking to me from the parking lot of a mall, from the sidewalk in front of the bank. The unmistakable message is *You can't save the world. That's my job.*

To be honest, I probably need some help. Professional help. Not that I have a problem with others getting counseling—but for me? I have my excuses. But I make an appointment.

Now that I'm seeing someone, I'm sorry I waited so long. I was all prepared to understand how my spouse's problems affect me and how if he changed, then I'd get all better. But when the first thing this counselor suggested was that I read a book called *Boundaries: When to Say Yes, How to Say No, to Take Control of Your Life,* by Dr. Henry Cloud and Dr. John Townsend, I groaned, "I've heard about that book forever, but I'm quite sure It's full of advice I already know." However, I dutifully ordered it. As I began to read, I had to face how wrong I was.

Taking care of yourself by saying, "No, I can't," is a troublesome thought to those who think following Christ means you must take care of everyone's problems however small they are. I even try to take care of problems others don't even know they have. It is also problematic for those of us who see that our current culture broadly encourages us to be self-indulgent, self-focused, and to never restrict our pleasure.

I also read *Let Your Life Speak* by Parker Palmer and tried to listen with unbiased ears, as every so often it hit a homerun.

> Don't boundaries turn us from other-centeredness to self-centeredness? The answer is no. Appropriate boundaries actually increase our ability to care about others.
>
> What Christ calls us to isn't the same thing as saying yes to everyone and everything.
>
> Self-care is never a selfish act—it is simply good stewardship of the only gift I have, the gift I was put on earth to offer to others. Anytime we can listen to true self and give it the care it requires, we do so not only for ourselves but for the many others whose lives we touch.[1]

My brain must contain years of neurological entrenchment and an archive full of boundary violations. I don't know when to stop worrying about other people. Some of the more overwhelming questions are: "If I don't, who will? What will so-and-so think of me if I don't? I'm afraid I won't be respected or loved. Why did I start this pattern? Where does this trouble come from?"

As a child, I was filled with anxiety, obsessed about our house burning down. When my parents were gone and I was babysitting my five younger brothers and sisters, I constantly worried about the house catching on fire. It was bitter cold outside and our front door was frozen shut. How would I get them all out the back door if a fire started? I repeatedly checked the gas burners on the kitchen stove and warily watched our wood stove glow red hot.

As I sat on the hot pavement after falling in front of the bank, it suddenly occurred to me: Marcy needed to come back to our house with the receipts anyway, so what was I thinking? Well. Too often I follow a path of trying to rescue people from their house fires, even if they aren't real.

This is *not* what Christ requires of me. He often left the multitudes and all their needs behind for various reasons. This path is my own, designed to relieve irrational fears. It's more about myself than you and that smarts. It's not the path God has designed.

Learning to say no to good things so we can say yes to what God has called us to do requires clarification. It poses lots of questions. What then ought we to be doing? How do we take care of ourselves properly? Does that care include rest and play? I'm listening with expectation. I've been given a rare chance to change at an age when we are prone to calcification.

A GENTLE MADNESS

WINTER 2014

> People have always collected things. Whether a vestige of our hunter-gatherer days, a need to forge order amid chaos, or a simple desire to have and to hold, the urge to possess is a hallmark of the human psyche. Yet pathology is a danger. Compulsive hoarders find value in everything. Others fixate on a single thing, succumbing to what author Nicholas Basbanes calls "a gentle madness." In 1869 the bibliophile Sir Thomas Phillipps said he needed "to have a copy of every book in the world." His final tally (50,000 books, perhaps 100,000 manuscripts) wasn't bad.[1]

As we prepare for a move we pray happens later this year, we are looking into closets, corners, and other hidey-holes in the house. What to sell, pitch, or move? Denis and I each have collections we think indicate pathology or at least a "gentle madness" in the other. He has too many books, and I have too many containers of unidentifiable organic stuffs in the refrigerator. He accuses me of housing colonies of cholera—little does he know that that gelatinous mass makes kombucha tea and could improve his health, if only he would drink it.

But, I ask, shouldn't some of his books go away, especially titles which no one, not even he, will crack open again? We have twenty-three bookcases packed full! At one point he reluctantly agreed to get rid of most of them. I know it hurt because they are his friends, but he had steeled himself. When our Board of Directors learned about this plan, one (who won't be named), in the time it takes to wave a hand, dismissed the idea, saying Denis should keep them! Otherwise, how would he do research? Several others agreed. Check. Mate. Perhaps they will help us move.

Still, I don't think seven thousand books compare to the refrigerator Denis frequently visits trying to sneak things into the trash without my knowing. Things I'm saving. Like creamy horseradish sauce, pepperoncini, capers, fish sauce, Angostura bitters (what are they for, anyway?)... all these necessary ingredients for that wonderful something I might make some day. When I catch him with his head in a shelf crying, "What's this? You never use it! It looks like rotten raccoon carcass! I'm throwing it out!" NOOOOO. That's like me throwing away all the obscure titles Francis Schaeffer wrote over the years. No. Do not throw away my fermented carrot condiment which I made and which I may or may not begin eating every day for the microbial health of my intestines.

Little by little, we have begun to sift through thirty-three years of homemaking at Toad Hall. Today, in early January, I'm going through my filing cabinet. Back, back into the dark ages of my life. Dumping, dumping. Throwing files of essays, clippings, reviews. Articles about children's authors. Crocheted blanket patterns. Bank loans. Pathetic poems by Margie. Trying not to stop and read and wonder: What was I thinking? It is easier to declutter and pitch when I remember that I'm lightening the load my children will one day haul to the trash. It will be one less box to handle when I die. I don't think my death is imminent, but I'm motivated.

It's more difficult to know what to do with the jewelry boxes that belonged to Denis' Aunt B and Aunt Ruth. Fake pearls, pop-beads, paste diamonds, heavy bracelets. Strangely configured brooches. Nothing of much value. Is there a granddaughter who would love these things? Perhaps turn them into glittering sculptures? Add them to vintage clothing? I don't know.

So, through the house I go, from the attic to the basement, sorting, deciding. A few items sold on craigslist, others posted "free," some taken to Salvation Army. I know this purging is doing me good because when the single bedspreads and button collections are gone, I feel freer, lighter.

We laugh about these things, but underneath I'm anxious. How will we manage the future? Why does every little thing need to be a hurdle of spiritual growth for me? It seems as if I am constantly being prodded to reach a level of maturity I can't achieve—that elusive place where I finally trust fully in God's interest in all my un-historic struggles. I constantly stray.

If things go as planned, by early March we will be ready for the 360-degree "show-off-the-home" show with bare surfaces and artfully placed bowls of fresh fruit. Our house will look as if no human has ever put their feet on a coffee table. It will never look better, but don't you dare believe we live like that every day. When we're finally listed—watch our Facebook pages for the MLS listing and you might be able to visit us at Toad Hall for the last time. I know that over the years many of you have wished you could stop in. We do, too. I would have had every one of you, if it were possible.

Two weeks later, we're back from our annual Board Meeting. This year it was in Chicago at Donald and Mary Guthrie's. Our directors are all old friends, peers who know and love us well. We've all been through much together. Their role in our ministry and lives seems to involve three things in varying degrees: Directing. Consulting. Blessing. We trust them.

In our discussions this year, as Denis and I outlined what we think of as the next phase of life—a gradual reduction of some responsibilities over a period of years, a move to a home on one level, and a look at what increased writing might involve—the Board sharpened their focus and tackled the question of *where*. We had been looking in an area north of Minneapolis and St. Paul. A rural area where we might own several acres and to tell the truth? It's sort of in the middle of nowhere. The questions they piled on boiled down to: what and who are you moving to?

Well, we're moving to Margie's dream: to expansive horizons with birds and wild animals. To gardens and no traffic or helicopters. To quiet beauty. Denis was with me in this, but he had fewer non-negotiables on the table.

I don't know how it happened that I determined we should move to "Nowhere Farm," because we have often advised people about where to move when they faced a big change. We say you must not move without considering where and who your community will be. What church or body of Christians will you become a part of? Who are the people who will be your friends? Everyone ought to have people with whom to develop deeper relationships—more than just a friendly wave at the checkout counter or a "peace be with you" at the appointed hour in church.

Back home, we are still processing, and I'm trying to understand how I could have blown past all my own advice. In her book, *Another Country*, Mary Pipher[2] warns people our age not to move to some exotic location that, though we've always dreamed of living there, is far from our community of friends and family—those who would surround us with help when our health disintegrates and we're deeply in need (that phrase scares me; I don't want to be deeply in need). Community trumps location in Pipher's mind. I didn't think I was ignoring her advice. It's not like it was the Florida Keys or Flathead County, Montana. But rural Minnesota is still pretty dreamy. But then I'm forced to imagine it: think of me being seventy-six (in ten years!). It's thirty below. The porch is sheeted in ice. The car won't start. Denis is sick. And we live forty-five miles from the ER in St. Paul.

Then there's Anita. She's been with us for almost six years now as our assistant, and her work has been incalculable. She has owned many things; she doesn't just complete a list of duties, but she comes alongside with her own initiative and gifts. But lately, she, too, has sensed a need for change. We love one another, so that isn't the reason for wanting new direction. She and I share a lot of interests, and I fantasized breathing about fresh air while she did the chores, raised chickens, and mended fences. Yes, I imagined her still doing all her Ransom work, too. It's embarrassing to admit I willfully ignored her signals about needing change, and the Board's suggestions that when we move, we need to look for a place where we could live minus what Anita can do, because in the near future she may need to find a different position for many good reasons.

As for what's to become of my dream? I am emotional about it. And confused—feeling one thing now and the opposite the next day. On one level, I'm quick to accommodate. That's what I did at our Board meeting when pressed about where we should live. I immediately saw my inconsistency. Then, as the people-pleaser I am, I quickly moved from my dream to saying, yeah, I could live here with a narrow little view in a Chicago suburb. So, fine. Give me a row house with a microchip yard.

On another level, I'm annoyed with God. Why doesn't he just give me what I want with a lot less fuss? I've worked hard all my life. I deserve this little piece of cake. This is embarrassing because I often process things verbally. So after blabbing (like I'm doing here), everyone knows what I'm thinking. When I change my mind, I have to go back and say, *Oh, sorry, that's not what I meant*, or *That's not going to happen*. Not even close. So here I am, willing to acknowledge a place in the country won't be likely.

As often as I return to J.I. Packer's wise words, they remind me of God's love:

> God is constantly taking knowledge of me in love . . . no discovery now can disillusion him about me, in the way I am so often disillusioned about myself, and quench his determination to bless me.[3]

We have lived through many crises and changes and have seen how faithfully God delivers us time after time, year after year, in ways I couldn't have imagined. But I still can't confidently shout: "Don't worry about where you'll live or *what you will wear*." Or as the *The Message* puts it:

> Don't fuss about what's on the table at mealtimes or if the clothes in your closet are in fashion. There is far more to your inner life than the food you put in your stomach, more to your outer appearance than the clothes you hang on your body. Look at the ravens, free and unfettered, not tied down to a job description, carefree in the care of God. And you count far more. (Luke 12:24)

I know it. I know it. I know it. But, God help me, I can still doubt. I don't know where Home is!

A prayer from Common Prayer touched my cloudy eyes today:

> We are blind to love, to justice, to grace, and to life. Help us not to condemn one another in our blindness, but rather to work together to help one another see more clearly by your light.[4]

I am so grateful that I haven't been condemned by the members of our Board for my blindness. I'd even be happy if I didn't condemn myself for blindness.

People don't normally write about things such as this in their ministry newsletters. It seems, well, *un*spiritual. However, declaring it unspiritual is antithetical to all we've stood for over the years. We maintain that there is not one square inch of life over which Christ does not reign. So all this dilemma and fogginess is part of our being human, struggling with our own faultiness and finiteness. It is exactly what God wants to take us through right now, even though I hate living with this uncertainty.

In some corner of my heart, I can give my hopes and dreams to God for safekeeping. I don't know where we will be in six months. I know there could be a spot for us that is more urban yet doesn't rule out a clear horizon and a quiet neighborhood. And if not? Will I eventually find grace and contentment in where we land? I think so.

I'm going to watch to see how all this turns out. In the meantime, if any of you understand just a portion of this—if you have lived counting down the days to some inevitable change in your life, uncertain of what will be, then I'm comforted. You can pray for us. You are my friend.

> Lord, to laugh in the midst of trial and to rejoice in the darkest valley is another way of saying, "Our hope is in you." Fill us with laughter and joy while we work for peace and strive for justice. Amen.[5]

SPRING, PLEASE COME

SUMMER 2014

We live in a climate where the seasons are sharp. There is no mistaking them. Winter freezes everything including our senses, but they waken again with the shifting south wind, with the slight rises in temps, with the clouds changing from steel gray to white muslin. When it is still well below freezing, we sniff the air and say, "I smell spring!" Chickadees add whistles to their dee-dee-deeing. Did you know that in spring, woodpeckers tap mating calls on hollow trees? They do. We heard them drumming today. Little feathered lovers calling to one another. Our eaves drip; long swords of ice hang from the roof. Trickles have turned into brooks running down alleys and sidewalks. Beneath the street a river rushes through the storm sewer on its way to the Mississippi. Winter drove frost deep into the ground, so deep that city water lines are freezing. (By regulation they are buried between six and seven feet deep.) Last night another ten inches of new snow fell.

This year more than ever, I want spring. I want hope to waken me hard and strong. Please come. Please bring sunshine and an easy green path to walk. Not that I've earned it. I know that. Despite our failures we are invited to bring all prayers to God, even the begging kind. There is one proviso: do it with thanksgiving (Phil. 4:6). I need a house.

So, Denis and I sat down for a little chat. His reasoning skills are sharper than mine, but my emotional quotient is above average. As long as we stay on the same side, we make a pretty good team. When it comes to selling our home and finding a new one, we must, of all things, be rational. Realistic. At the same time, we agree to reserve some optimism for a place of quietness and beauty with space for breathing and looking at the sky and being in the city. That would be prime.

He says, "It's like this. Our present home, with two floors, is 2,400 square feet minus Mole's End, the little studio where Anita lives. The basement that is finished and houses my library and the laundry room add more square feet. Now. It looks as if the sale of our home, after real estate expenses and what not, will leave us with enough to purchase a home a little less than half that size in the Twin Cities area. So we need to think about how to reduce our belongings so they fit in about one thousand square feet of space." *What?* What is he saying?

With all my heart I want to do this move well, but as he speaks I have a mounting sense of panic. I see truckloads of furniture being pitched over a cliff. I have the urge to stop my ears and run away, hugging my oak cabinets and pottery bowls to my chest. Why is it that little ramblers with wall-to-wall carpet in 80s deco make me want to weep? But this must be faced. We need, for one thing, most rooms on the main floor. Denis brings a glass of wine and sits beside me on the couch. "We can do this," he asserts. "It will be hard. Painful. But it is what people must do at our stage of life. We have always believed there are ways of living creatively, of being hospitable. Space does not limit these things."

True. True. All true. But what about the view I've longed for? The beauty of nature surrounding me? Should I give it up? Perhaps. I go to the public library and find books with beautiful pictures and tips for living in small spaces. It helps a little.

The following week, Anita and I get our house staged for photos. Carol, the real estate agent's wife, walks through, telling us what to put away. That chair, the chopping block, everything off the refrigerator, no throw rugs, that footstool, your living room blankies—the list goes on. Luckily, we have an attic with lots of room and Anita is small but strong. Everyday Denis looks a little more shocked. "It's so barren," he moans. But I'm starting to like it. Clean surfaces, no clutter. Even the radiators are dusted. Wow. Toad Hall has never looked this unlived in. Gradually, he becomes more used to it, and I'm more receptive to the idea that when we move less could be more. Perhaps.

A few days later, the young man who does real estate pics arrives. He says our house is easy to shoot, and he loves the feel of it. It's inviting. Lots of light. Warm colors. As he leaves, he spontaneously bursts, "I would buy this if I could." I'm absurdly pleased. A complete stranger likes our house? Perhaps it will sell after all.

Now it's Friday and the listing goes live tonight. We pray about the things beyond our control. We pray for the right buyer, the timing, perhaps for a family that would love the house as we have.

Saturday is quiet all day and feels like we are waiting for a glacier to calve. The "For Sale" sign on the front lawn looks so wrong. *What* were we thinking? Perhaps I should take it down. On Sunday we are gone all day. But that's when calls to show the house start coming in. For the next three days, lookers pour through. I imagine people jumping on our beds and opening the medicine cabinet to examine our prescriptions. Normal paranoia.

Tuesday. We haven't done a lick of work because we must rush around every other second putting away ratty towels, smoothing lumps on beds, grabbing laptops, and leaving in a flurry. (This is the downside of having your offices at home when trying to sell your house.) It's only been on the market three days, but in the afternoon, we receive four offers and must decide on one of them by evening. Our agent is awesomely efficient and professional—another answer to our prayers for finding an honest, trustworthy person. One offer is from a family who is offering more than our asking price and a good closing date. They love the house and want their mother to live with them! Anita's apartment in Mole's End will be perfect for her. We accept, and the "SOLD" sign goes up.

We can't believe how fast this has happened. Our doubts are dispelled and our trust in God rises. We immediately relax our housekeeping and return to our slovenly ways. Dirty socks on the floor and Honeysuckle hopping through the house, dropping little pellets here and there. (Yes. Well. They are hard little things that are barely discernable on the carpets. In fact, Anita accidentally ate one once. She was sitting on the couch eating raisins and watching TV when she dropped one and without looking down, she reached to the floor, felt around, picked it up, popped it in her mouth thinking... But I digress.)

Next comes the hard part. We *need* to find a new home. There is no turning back.

We feel God's nearness to our almost homeless condition. We are in a stage of life Mary Pipher[1] calls the "young-old." Whether we like it or not, when you are in your sixties, you are no longer middle-aged. Sorry, Baby Boomers. We move from "young-old" to "old-old" when we face a crisis that moves us from the kingdom of the well to the kingdom of the sick. A mate dies; a fall breaks a hip; a test for cancer comes back positive What stays the same is our Shepherd who loves us whether young or old, pregnant or barren, swift or slowly limping along. Somewhere in my bones, I know this beyond a doubt.

Pipher writes,

> My bias is that luxurious surroundings, entertainment options, natural beauty, and good weather are less important than people. As songwriter Greg Brown said, "You can't have a cup of coffee with the landscape." At bottom, I think the search for the right place is a search for the right people. It's a search for love and respect. What's important is a community of friends and family.[2]

As much as I would like a mountain cabin or cottage by the sea, I remember the encouragement of our Board of Directors[3] to consider community—what we're moving to, not just where we're moving.

Putting the isolated country home dream aside, we visited a few churches in the Twin Cities exploring possibilities. Could we find a church home, and *then* locate a place to live? One Sunday, we visited a church that was a joyful experience for both of us. The place seemed so God-ordained for us, I wept through the entire service. There seemed real potential for community and friends. Another important piece fell into place.

We have talked endlessly about what Home could look like for us—what kind of hospitality will we offer there? What kind of quiet do we need for more serious writing days? What constitutes an okay amount of solitude? How much comfort are we allowed to enjoy? As we searched, I had to confess that the outside of a house either immediately draws me in or repels me. Architect Sarah Susanka writes, "The house embodies in its exterior form much of what we long for today—a house that says Home before you ever step through the door."[4] Most newly-constructed houses with the giant three-car garage in front don't call "Home" to me. I have drafted and re-drafted our list of non-negotiables. Perhaps we should begin crossing them off, when so many in the world suffer from homelessless.

With our house sold and a church in view, we are now more focused on finding the right location for our new house. I don't want you to think we believe that if you do things right—speak the right words, pray the right prayers—then your house will sell, you'll find a church you like, and God will give you waffles for breakfast every morning. No. The Bible does not teach us that.

There are no possibilities right now. There are very few homes on the market in the Twin Cities and good ones get snapped up immediately. Moving to a rental while we find the right one? Just kill me now. A friend jokes, "Buy an RV!" Another adds, you can name it "Road Hall!" Denis is adamant. The right one will be there at the right time. We have until June. We are dividing search responsibilities. Mine being approximately nothing—I get too fixated on flower boxes and countertop colors to be of much use. Denis and Anita do the research and I vote up or down. We try not to hit the pits on the same day.

A reader wrote regarding our move and the stress that will be a part of it:

> From reading some other Christian writers, I get the feeling that they experience a crisis in faith for "one whole night" while they throw up in the bathroom with the flu as a quadriplegic. But in the morning everything is bright and beautiful. I know that both of us can't be right, but it seems that these people are not being

> honest with themselves (or anyone else). They make me feel like a failure, but I do know that King David certainly had more ups and downs than they admit.
>
> —Paul S.

This process may take us longer than "one whole night" of vomiting on the floor. We may face temporary homelessness longer than I want to. I think about the three Old Testament men who were thrown into the furnace, who said "If God chooses, he can deliver us from death, but if he doesn't, he is still God and our faith is in him."

At my end of the scale, where mortal danger is embarrassingly low, it's still good to say the same thing. God can choose to give us the ideal home I have in my heart. Or not. And if not, God is still God, and I have faith that one day I will go Home—with a capital H. God has set us a direction and we're walking the path.

GOODBYE TOAD HALL

SUMMER 2014

A friend told me I would need to eat an enormous amount of crow after moaning about down-sizing to a thousand square feet, but back in March I had no idea we were going to have more flexibility than we imagined. We had just sold Toad Hall and were staggered that it had only been on the market for three days when we received four offers. All were more than our asking price. After much euphoria and relief, we were immediately under pressure to find a new place and get out of Toad Hall by July.

We knew a little about the buyers of Toad Hall. On a spring day after it sold, when the tulips were in bloom, we met the buyers' parents as they walked past our yard. They told us they had moved into our neighborhood in 1997 when their daughter was still in high school. They often passed our house and she always said, "I love that house. Someday I want it to be mine." She had never seen the inside, but our windows were often lit up in the evening and passersby could see the warm colors, coffee mugs on the rack, and artwork on the walls. Maybe that was part of what drew her. She grew up, left home, married, had children of her own, and lived in a nearby town. When our "For Sale" sign went up, her parents immediately called her. She quickly called our agent and said, "I want that house no matter the price!" Her husband was fine with the idea: he works for Mayo Clinic and our location was convenient for his work as well as for nearby grandparents, and (bonus!) Mole's End could be a place for the husband's mother to live. We listened to this remarkable story and could hardly believe how God had prepared this woman from the time she was a girl to be in the right place with the right finances to buy our home at the right time. It delights us to know it will be a home for another family to enjoy.

In February, we began looking throughout the Metro area of Minneapolis—educating ourselves about real estate and thinking about townhomes versus stand-alone houses. We plunged into the dark abyss of real estate marketing, spending hours and hours sorting through dozens and dozens of houses online where often the photos and descriptions had *nothing* to do with reality. We got so sick of it, sometimes we could barely turn on the computer without snarling. The market moved so fast we had to drive up to the Twin Cities several times a week, only to find that in the hours before we arrived, what we only wanted to *look* at was already sold. Or we'd arrive at an address that looked perfect on paper to find it was next to a Walmart parking lot. Every week I talked about giving up our non-negotiables (like a quiet neighborhood, or a guest room) and Denis would say no, let's keep praying and waiting.

On April 11th we found a house that, to me, looked boring on the outside; in fact, when we drove up, I didn't want to go in. But Denis convinced me that since our agent had made arrangements to see it I must cooperate. Inside, the house bloomed with potential. It was in our price range, on a quiet street, and backed up to a forty-six acre park. It had a main floor bedroom, bath, and laundry—good for old folks who can't climb stairs as body parts begin to fail. At the back of the house was a beautiful sunroom with large windows on three sides, perfect for my office, almost like being in a tree house. Right above it on the second floor was its exact twin. Who would build a house with *two* sunrooms? It had less square footage than Toad Hall, but felt more spacious because of the open floor plan and the second floor loft with a library overlooking the fireplace and living room.

We walked around thinking, how perfect is this? Our agent, surprised that it was still on the market, kept looking for the big flaw, saying, "I can't see *anything* wrong with this house! It just has to be under the radar!" *Or, perhaps,* we thought, *it's been shielded from other eyes by God's providence?* We immediately wrote an offer and—confident that it would be ours and filled with excitement—stopped for dinner on the way back to Rochester to celebrate. On our drive home from the restaurant, we got the call: offer rejected. The irony of us jumping the gun to celebrate made us feel stupid and depressed.

We learned another buyer had been low-balling the sellers, but when he heard we made a higher offer, he quickly came in above ours. We were back to square one. So we kept on looking and finding nothing. Our board members tried to encourage us. Donald Guthrie said, "Just because the sellers accepted another offer doesn't mean it won't fall through. I'm praying it will." Ed Hague tried to make us laugh saying: "You haven't suffered enough and I didn't like the front of the house anyway." That didn't work. Day after day, Denis kept repeating; "But that house is *ours*, don't they *know* that?" He-who-never-dreams even dreamt the house belonged to us. I wanted to believe his dream was prophetic. In an abnormal role reversal, he maintained that we needed to wait and see, while I prepared for worst-case scenarios.

Three weeks later, we heard from our agent. The house was back on the market after the inspection and the potential buyers had backed out. We resubmitted our offer. The next day it was rejected again because the buyers had repented and decided to go ahead. Argh! Two days later our agent called *again*. He told us the listing agent was so embarrassed she made her husband call him to ask if those people from Rochester would consider coming in again, because, once again, the sale was off and the sellers were now so mad at the other party they weren't going to sell to the "buyers from hell" no matter what they offered. So once more we were ready to go and this time it was magic. The house was ours! We celebrated with shouts of joy and huge sighs of relief. No time for frivolous dinners now, because suddenly the new closing date of May 30th was coming up smoking fast.

Speaking of smoking, our house is in Savage, MN, a little community just south of the Twin Cities. The word "Savage" makes us think of burning and pillaging. I am Norwegian, and after all, my ancestors, the Vikings, were pretty good at this.

We hired a local moving company to load and unload us. The owner was young, but experienced. Maybe not experienced enough, though. He gave us a ridiculously low estimate and thought it might take four hours and two trucks to load up our house. It took three trucks and nine hours, and oh, it was a hot, humid day! On the way to Savage, one of his trucks broke down and had to be towed back to Rochester, unloaded and reloaded and brought to us the next day. Thankfully, our beds were in the first truck to arrive. The crew was wonderful; it was a pleasure to keep them hydrated and fed with pizza. As I watched the young men work so hard, I was astounded. I've completely forgotten what it's like to have energy at the end of a long day, enough so you can bounce up the ramp, playfully jump up to hit a strap hanging from the roof of the truck, pick up two boxes of books weighing fifty pounds each, and carry them into the house. So many boxes were labeled "Anita's crafts"—filled with her supplies and tools—that one of them asked, "So, Anita works for you, right? Do you pay her money or do you just give her Hobby Lobby gift certificates?"

On the outside, our new home is not so photogenic as Toad Hall. It has more of an inner beauty, as the space opens up inside and draws you in. Each morning I step out of our bedroom, look across the kitchen, past the dining room, and see my office lit up as the rising sun shines across the room. We look out the back of the house onto a canopy of trees and a wooded ravine that rises up to our backyard with long stretches of grass on either side. On certain days we can hear the hidden stream that bubbles and flows through the valley below. There is carpet in many rooms, even the dining area—who would do that?—but I'm surprised to enjoy padding quietly about. Unlike the oak stairs at Toad Hall, which creaked and groaned on every step so that not even the stealthiest visitor could creep up them, these wide stairs are carpeted. Here, I could easily sneak up on Denis in his office and scare him half to death, but I won't.

It has been such a gift—the beauty, the way the house functions, its layout, the peacefulness. The atmosphere is sort of cabin-y—with a restful, retreat-like feel. Every day we recognize God's hand in the way events unfolded; all this grace poured out despite my doubts of ever finding something we would love. Every day we thank him for some new thing we hadn't noticed. Flower beds that need weeding, yes, but are full of potential. Birds that sing like crazy. All the utility lines are buried. Not once has a helicopter thundered over. There is no traffic in this court. In fact, late one night, the lights of a car flashed through our bedroom and I got up to see what that was all about. We are seeing wildlife. Deer. Turkeys. Birds at our feeder. One morning a fox curled up on the driveway.

We have christened this home "The House Between." We don't know the number of days or years we have yet to live, but it is possible this will be our last house. Thus, it exists in the time between the now and what will one day become our permanent Home when we go to be with God.

I have wondered how to write this issue of *Notes From Toad Hall,* which will now be called *Letters from the House Between*, and how to report on all that has happened. Please understand our story is not meant to be a standard, as if you pray, wait, and be thankful, then God will give you what you want. If I'm not careful, that may be how it sounds. He gives to his children, not based on our good attitude (mine is almost always lacking) or good work (very spotty in my case), but according to his plans and purposes so that we may learn how better to love and serve him.

5:00 a.m. The birds are raising a clamor. Not just one or two robins and a single cardinal, but a multitude. Birdsong I don't recognize, like the little two-part squeak, repeated over and over. We feel uncommonly blessed. There is so much behind us. We are free from stress for a while. With joy we anticipate this stage—the people, a church we love, and quiet with more space in which to write.

So here I sit in my office, books open, and my computer charged. The sun streams in from the east. Coffee beside me. I know the word that wants out of my soul: unclench.

> By awesome deeds you answer us with righteousness, O God of our salvation, the hope of all the ends of the earth and of the farthest seas . . . those who dwell at the ends of the earth are in awe at your signs. You make the going out of the morning and the evening to shout for joy . . . you crown the year with your bounty; your wagon tracks overflow with abundance. The pastures of the wilderness overflow, the hills gird themselves with joy, the meadows clothe themselves with flocks, the valleys deck themselves with grain, they shout and sing together for joy (Psalm 65:5, 8, 11–13 ESV).

EPILOGUE

FALL 2020

All around us our world is in grief, turmoil, and want. I do not plan to avoid it by staying safely within my little bubble. I want to rejoice in God's power that keeps the entire universe in his hands, from the smallest virus to the most wicked dictator. This, right along with the small and the beautiful, like the spotted fawn that wandered through our yard yesterday following her graceful mother. I want to keep learning what God is up to in the lives of others, because so often it's something I never would have imagined or thought to do myself. That is glorious.

Someone may legitimately ask why, here in this final book of the trilogy, are even more of the stories from your spiritual pilgrimage? It may look egotistical or self-absorbed to think anyone wants to hear about my little peccadillos and minor victories, but they are the stories of my life, of our life as a couple, as a family, as custodians of the gifts we've been given.

There are good reasons for sharing them. One is the desire to leave a spiritual legacy. Daniel Taylor has put this into words far better than I could. "Telling your stories is the central act of a spiritual legacy. It is not a self-indulgence or a passing entertainment. As part of a spiritual legacy, telling your stories is the fulfillment of a responsibility—the responsibility to pass on wisdom. It doesn't matter whether you feel you have wisdom—your stories do."[1]

Frederick Buechner affirms this when he writes: "To lose track of our stories is to be profoundly impoverished not only humanly but also spiritually."[2]

If I write my stories anywhere near well, then through them you will recognize yourself and see that my story is your story, too. It is deeply touching that often, through our stories, we encounter God, who has made himself known to us in a personal and powerful way. Suddenly, the light turns on and we see that we share in some universal experience of what it means to be human and finite.

Another important reason I've spent these many years writing is the teachings about the Victorious Christian Life that appear in many forms in the church through sermons, books, and radio programs. From early on I understood that if, as a Christian, you were faithful, you would overcome all sin and adversity. You would be, successful, trouble-free and happy. Wealth, education, and health were signs of this.

One of our grandsons who is temporarily staying with us shared something that made me proud of him and yet saddened me. With insight beyond his years, he recounted how when he was a student in a Christian middle school, it was taught both explicitly and implied that if you were blessed by God, you would, as he put it, "live in really nice homes, drive new cars, be rich, and everything about you and your family would be great." That is not how life was for him. His family was not making it financially, their car needed repairs, there were injuries and sicknesses, and worst of all, his family was falling apart.

I asked him if he had any idea what could be the long term effect of this teaching. He thought that when kids face trouble, which they inevitably will, they will be surprised and unprepared, and they could lose their faith.

When I was younger, I faced struggles no one else seemed to have. I wondered, why? It looked as though everyone else's marriages were perfect. All their decisions were exactly right. No one ever doubted the goodness of God. I wondered why I failed to live up to the standards I set for myself, to say nothing of God's demands. I felt alone in my struggles and doubts.

As I grew older and more experienced, I learned that many Christians faced similar struggles, but we often hid our problems because we felt we were not supposed to have them in the first place. We were supposed to be Victorious Christians.

Knowing we are not alone in the struggles we face; knowing how many times I have picked myself up, dusted off my pants and kept going. Knowing God has told us to expect suffering, but also that he will be with us in the midst of it: this is why I share my life's stories. I want you to be encouraged in your quest for godliness. I want to remind you that you are not alone. For Christ's sake and because he has commanded it, we must share our burdens with one another, not hide them.

Again and again I return to one of my favorite quotes by J.I. Packer in order to be reminded that God is for us.

> There is unspeakable comfort—the sort of comfort that energizes, . . . in knowing that God is constantly taking knowledge of me in love, and watching over me for my good. There is tremendous relief in knowing that his love to me is utterly realistic, based at every point on prior knowledge of the worst

> about me, so that no discovery now can disillusion him about me, in the way I am so often disillusioned about myself, and quench his determination to bless me.[3]

As I see it, Denis and I are living the final stage of our life together. I don't know how long that will last nor what life will look like in the future. I have followed God across the years and across the continent. Sometimes I have stumbled, but he bears me up, and I will continue to follow him into the unknown.

I will continue watching to see what God is doing in my own ordinary life. I want to honestly face growing older, more infirm, and more dependent on others. Now that I am somewhere near the end, I would like to keep sharing stories of God's continued grace and work in my life, in our life together.

With this in mind, I send into the world these small bits of life and wisdom that have been gathered over the years. I hope that through them others will find something relevant to their own pilgrimage and be blessed.

RECIPES

PEASANT FOOD

Over the years we hosted hundreds of people around our table with a desire to gather them in, to love and feed them. Sharing a meal is only part of what it means to show hospitality, a virtue that is found throughout the Christian scriptures and among all the early church fathers and mothers. By feeding others we meant to demonstrate that we cared about the health of their hearts as much as we cared for physical needs. For us it never became an effort to entertain, but to serve. It was seldom dramatic or noteworthy, but rather it was ridiculously homespun. Wade Bradshaw writes in *by demonstration: God,* "The trick of real hospitality is not always to make a special time of the meal but to include people in it naturally. We should include others in what we do and drop entirely the effort to impress them."

This is what motivated us. At the same time, I admit that cooking is not only something I enjoy doing, it is a form of creativity. I often ask myself what can I make that would nourish and delight this person? What can we do to create a welcoming and safe atmosphere around the table, and also make it beautiful? It seemed to work because on many occasions our guests, who often became dear friends, felt free to share their longings, their history, and even their secrets. In the midst of laughter and talking there were often tears, so we learned to keep a box of tissue handy. That, too, became a part of our meal and conversations. Denis and I sometimes joked with one another that we had the gift of making people cry. Over time we learned this was not a bad thing. On the contrary, we had established a place that not only welcomed and fed, but disarmed and sheltered people who felt free to share their hearts with us. It was a privilege. An honor to be there with them.

All these recipes we ate at Toad Hall and later at The House Between are time-honored favorites of our family and friends. Many of them are quite simple, which can be a good thing. I have a friend who is a wonderful gourmet cook, and I've enjoyed many of her creations. Her dishes are often complex and unusual, but always beautiful and wonderfully tasty. By comparison, I'm more of a peasant-style cook. I love making food that is comforting, often simple, and a lot of it. There is room for both of us.

I encourage everyone, not just women or married persons but also men and singles to find simple but delectable dishes you can make and share. Perhaps you will find one here. Keep in mind that as you prepare and serve you are doing far more than meeting physical needs, you are serving Jesus by expressing love and a desire to minister to hearts, not just bodies. Finally, don't be discouraged by failures, I've had plenty. Experience helps, but even as seasoned as I am, I can still botch a dish in some way.

Apple Puff Pancake is a recipe I am so fond of I could eat it every day for breakfast. Of course, one shouldn't do that because it is rather desert-like. Though I happily share this with anyone who is around, there is no doubt when I make it, it is for myself. I make it when I feel discouraged, when I'm happy and energetic, and even when slightly sick. That translates into almost Any Time. It is best made with apples that like to hold their shape, such as Gala, Jonathan, Granny Smith, or Honeycrisp. This dish comes together easily and is great for a special breakfast treat. One caveat: puff? Mine are totally hit or miss on the puff part. I've tried to figure out why and have found no solution. No matter. It's always delicious.

Apple Puff Pancake in Cast Iron

3 tbsp butter
3 apples, peeled and sliced
1/4 cup brown sugar
1/2 tsp cinnamon
2 eggs
3/4 cup milk
1/2 tsp salt
1 tbsp sugar
3/4 cup flour

Heat oven to 450 degrees.

Melt butter in a cast-iron Dutch oven *(or a ceramic pot that can be used on the burner as well as the oven)*. Make sure the butter reaches up the sides. Turn the heat up to medium and add the apples with brown sugar and cinnamon.

Saute until the apples begin to soften and caramelize. *(You don't want them all the way caramelized because the process will continue in the oven.)* While the apples are cooking whisk together the milk, eggs, sugar, and salt.

Add flour to the liquid and whisk just until smooth.

Pour over the apples and place in oven.

Bake for 15–18 minutes until puffy and the edges are a little browned.

Drizzle each serving with a little maple syrup.

Makes 3–4 servings.

This breakfast dish for a special day is easy, economical and, impressive. It makes a wonderful gift to drop by a friend who could use some extra comfort or help.

Caramel French Toast

1/2 cup melted butter
1 cup brown sugar
1/2 tsp cinnamon
English muffin bread *(fits perfectly in a 9 x 13-inch pan)*
6 eggs
1 1/2 cups milk
1/2 tsp salt

Melt the butter directly in the pan. Rotate so butter spreads around.

Add brown sugar and cinnamon to the pan and stir it into the butter.

Place two slices of bread on top of one another. Repeat until the whole bottom is covered with stacks of bread.

In a bowl whisk together eggs, milk, and salt. Pour over bread.

Refrigerate overnight. *(In a pinch, a couple hours will do if you rise early.)*

Bake at 350 degrees for 25–30 minutes, or until the top is puffed up and the edges are brown and crispy. You can also check doneness by inserting a knife in the middle to see if it has set.

Optional: Serve with maple syrup.

There are many cornbread recipes out there, but this one has the power to convert cornbread haters into lovers. Some recipes are unappetizing because they are dry enough to make you choke. This one never fails, it is always tender and moist. Using fresh ground organic corn meal enhances the flavor.

Cornbread

1 cup flour
1 cup cornmeal
3/4 tsp salt
4 tsp baking powder
2 eggs
1 cup milk
1/4 cup cooking oil
1/4 cup honey *(or substitute 1/2 cup sugar)*

Mix the dry ingredients together in a mixing bowl.

Add eggs, milk, honey, and oil. Beat or whisk just until smooth. There may be some lumps.

Pour into a greased 8" square pan or pie plate.

Bake at 375 degrees for 25 minutes until done in the middle.

4-5 servings. *(This recipe is easily doubled and baked in a 13 x 9 inch pan.)*

March is a gloomy month in Minnesota. By then we are all sick of winter and yet spring may still be a month and a half away. Irish Soda Bread is always cranked out of my kitchen around Saint Patrick's Day. It is a delicious way to fill your kitchen with the enticing scent of fresh baked bread and cheer the most morose soul. Irish Soda Bread is made with simple ingredients and only requires a little kneading. Leftovers are great toasted and spread with honey or jam. It makes a lovely gift to lift the spirits of a friend or neighbor.

Irish Soda Bread

4 cups unbleached, all-purpose flour
4 tbsp sugar
1 tbsp baking powder
1 tsp baking soda
1/2 tsp salt
1 cup raisins or currants
1/2 cup butter softened
1 cup buttermilk (plus 1/4 cup buttermilk—see note)
1 egg
1/4 cup butter, melted

Preheat oven to 375 degrees.

Lightly grease a baking sheet or use parchment paper to line it.

In a large bowl, mix together flour, sugar, baking soda, baking powder, salt, and raisins. Add butter and incorporate with a fork. Stir in 1 cup buttermilk and egg.

Turn dough onto a floured surface and knead slightly with hands until you can form it into a ball. Place it on the baking sheet to make one large loaf, or cut it in half to make two smaller loaves. Use a knife to cut an "X" into the top of the loaf. In a small bowl, combine the melted butter and remaining buttermilk and brush the top of the loaf. Bake for 45–50 minutes or until a toothpick comes out clean.

Note: Be sure to purchase lowfat buttermilk. It works better than nonfat. Buttermilk has more uses than you may think. It is great to keep around for pancakes and biscuits. It stores for a long time in the refrigerator. I've kept it for up to six weeks. If you don't have buttermilk on hand, make a substitute by souring milk. Add 1 tbsp of white vinegar or lemon juice to 1 cup milk. Don't be afraid of "sour." You can't taste it in the final product but it is an important addition to the recipe.

My favorite recipe for scones makes a slightly sweet pastry that has a kind of biscuit-y texture. These scones get a little crisp on the bottom and golden on top. I want resistance when I bite down—not an unfrosted piece of cake or soft cookie like many I've tried. The following recipe appeared in our local newspaper years ago and was posted by a woman who owned a bakery. I loved her scones, and when she shared the recipe it became one of my all-time favorite breakfast pastries.

Daube's Scones

3 1/2 cups unsifted flour
1/2 cup sugar
1 tbsp plus 1 1/2 tsp baking powder
1 tsp salt
1/2 cup cold butter
1/2 cup raisins *(or currants, or other dried fruit)*
1 tbsp grated lemon peel, or to taste
2 large eggs
3/4 cup cream
1/4 cup milk

Preheat oven to 400 degrees.

In a large bowl mix flour, sugar, baking powder, and salt.

With a pastry blender cut in the butter until the dough looks like coarse cornmeal.

Stir in raisins and lemon peel.

In a small bowl whisk eggs, cream, and milk. Add to the flour mixture, stirring quickly with a fork until dough leaves side of bowl. Press with hands to make a ball.

On a well-floured surface, roll dough to about 3/4 inch thickness in a 9-inch round.

Use a round biscuit cutter or another shape to cut dough. Or simply cut it into about 10–12 wedges according to how big you want them.

Place scones on ungreased baking sheet or parchment.

Optional: Sprinkle tops with a cinnamon, sugar mix.

Bake 12–15 minutes or until golden. Remove to a wire rack. Immediately brush with honey.

When hot summer days arrive and the cucumbers multiply in pots on the deck so quickly I can't keep up with them, I think about serving this unusual, refreshing cold soup. Some of our guests have hesitated at first, feeling it was a little too weird to hold any merit. They often changed their minds after tasting it and asked for second helpings. It's that good.

Cold Cucumber Yogurt Soup

1 boiled egg, chopped
1/2 cup raisins
2–3 cups yogurt
1/2 cup light cream
6 ice cubes
1 medium to large cucumber, grated
1/4 cup green onions, chopped
2 tsp salt
1/2 tsp pepper
1 cup cold water
1 tbsp parsley, chopped
1 tbsp fresh dill, chopped

Soak raisins in cold water for 5 minutes. Drain.
Mix all ingredients together in large bowl or container.
Add raisins and 1 cup water.
Refrigerate 2–3 hours before serving.
Garnish each serving with parsley and dill.
Makes 4–5 servings. (Will keep for 2–3 days in the refrigerator.)

This soup is super easy to make and comes together in no time. It features lots of garlic. Olive oil is a must and you cannot skimp on it. It is a great soup to make when unexpected company shows up.

Kale and Cannellini Bean Soup

2 tbsp olive oil
6 cloves garlic, chopped
1 pound fresh kale, chopped
4 cups chicken broth
1 can cannellini beans, drained and rinsed
Grated Parmesan cheese
5 tbsp extra-virgin olive oil

Heat 2 tbsp olive oil in a large heavy pot over medium heat. Add garlic and saute until fragrant. *(This is a great vegetarian dish, but an option is adding sliced Italian sausage or other savory sausage to saute along with the garlic at the beginning.)*

Add kale and saute until wilted. *(I often blanch and freeze extra kale in the summer for this very soup which often appears during our long winter.)*

Add chicken broth, salt, pepper, beans, and Parmesan cheese.

Cover and simmer until soup is heated through. Adjust seasonings.

Add a generous amount of olive oil at the very end.

3–4 servings.

Our soups are popular in the cold months and most of them are classified as comfort food. They are all complete meals when you add a loaf of French bread and a dish of olives and pickles. This soup is very simple and comes together quickly. This recipe can be easily increased to make more servings or be kept for leftovers. When increasing, I use whatever leeks I have on hand and don't worry if there isn't quite enough for a double recipe. The flavor is always great.

Potato Leek Soup

3 leeks, sliced
4 medium potatoes *(I like Yukon Gold)*
4 cups chicken broth

1 cup milk *(half-and-half can be substituted for a portion of the milk if desired)*
Salt and pepper to taste
Garlic croutons *(optional)*

In a soup pot, saute leeks in butter over medium heat until softened.

Add peeled, diced potatoes and chicken broth. Simmer until potatoes are soft.

At this point you can mash the soup with a potato masher to make a somewhat chunky soup or blend until smooth with a hand held blender or in a food processor.

Add milk and adjust flavors. Heat but do not boil.

Serve with croutons.

Makes 4 servings.

This soup was a favorite of our Aunt Ruth (now deceased) who insisted she hated Mexican food and refused to admit this soup had anything to do with its origins. She claimed she would *never* eat Mexican food because she hated anything hot, and yet she devoured this slightly spicy soup. It is especially delicious when you make your own crispy tortilla chips to add crunch on top of the bowl.

Tortilla Soup

10 cups water
2 tbsp Better Than Bouillon, chicken *(or other form of bouillon)*
1 cup rice
1 small onion, diced
1/3 cup fresh lemon juice
2 tbsp sugar
1/2 tsp garlic powder *(substitute 2 cloves, chopped fine)*
1/2 tsp ground cumin
1/2 tsp salt
Pepper to taste
2 cans green chili
2 cans diced tomatoes
1 1/2 cups diced, cooked chicken
Tortilla chips
Grated cheese
Fresh cilantro, chopped
Sour cream *(optional)*

Bring water, bouillon, seasonings and rice to a boil. Simmer until rice is tender.

Add tomatoes, chili, and chicken. Heat but do not boil.

Taste and adjust flavor if needed.

Serves 4–6

To serve: Place in individual bowls. Top with cheese, cilantro, chips and sour cream.

NOTE: Make your own tortilla strips by cutting corn tortillas in strips and dropping them in hot oil. This is an extra step, but worth it. Fry until light golden, drain on paper towels and salt them. When I make chips I hide them until needed or they will all be eaten before the meal. Most are surprised at how much better these taste than the packaged variety.

The additional vegetables in this upgraded three bean salad increase its nutritional value and add color. This salad looks beautiful when served in a clear glass bowl. It will keep for up to a week when refrigerated and can be stored in glass jars. It has also has the power to convert folks who think they don't like this type of salad.

Calico Salad

4 medium carrots, sliced
1 can red kidney beans
1 can yellow wax beans
1 cup green beans *(I use frozen for a brighter color)*
1 can garbanzo beans
5 green onions, sliced
2 stalks celery, diced
1/3 cup sugar
1/3 wine vinegar
1/3 cup extra-virgin olive oil
1 tsp dry mustard
1 tsp salt
1/2 tsp pepper

Parboil carrots for five minutes. Drain, then place in ice water. Place carrots in a large bowl.

Add green beans *(if canned, drain first).*

Add remaining vegetables.

In a small bowl whisk together sugar, vinegar, oil, and spices. Pour over vegetables. Refrigerate for several hours before serving.

Serves 6–8.

NOTE: You can add any other canned beans or other fresh vegetables you think might be a good addition. Depending on how much more is added, increase the dressing a little to compensate.

This is a favorite chicken dish at our house. It's easy, and even pleases even my grandchildren whose tastes are somewhat limited.

Greek Chicken

1 whole chicken cut up in parts or 6–8 bone-in thighs
4–5 medium to large potatoes, cut into serving pieces
1/2 cup olive oil
Oregano
Salt

Heat oven to 375 degrees.

Generously salt the chicken on all sides and set aside while you prepare the potatoes.

Place potatoes in bottom of 9x13-inch baking pan and pour olive oil over them. (Don't skimp on this.) Make sure each piece is coated with oil. Sprinkle with more salt.

Place chicken skin side up on top of potatoes.

Sprinkle very generously with dried oregano.

Bake for 1 hour. (Be sure to test the potatoes for doneness before removing.)

Serves 5–6.

This meat marinade works especially well for pork, whether it is being grilled or roasted, but I have used it successfully with chicken and beef, too. This recipe calls for using a mortar and pestle which fills the air with lovely aromatic scents as you work.

Coriander Pepper Marinade

2 cloves garlic, crushed
1 tbsp crushed coriander seeds
8 crushed peppercorns
1 tbsp brown sugar
3 tbsp soy sauce *(I often use a lot more than the recipe calls for)*

Crush seeds and peppercorns in a mortar until broken.
Add garlic to the mortar and mash it into the spice.
Mix all ingredients together in a small bowl.
Place meat in a large ziplock bag.
Add marinade, close bag, and gently shake meat to coat on all sides.
Marinate for at least 30 minutes and up to 12 hours.

Rosemary Roast Chicken has been a standard in my kitchen for many years. I can't be convinced to roast a whole chicken any other way. The basting sauce does require a little extra effort, but it is more than worth it. As it roasts the scent will drive you crazy. Thanks to my oldest daughter for this gem.

Rosemary Roast Chicken

1 whole 3-4 pound chicken
2 tbsp olive oil
2 tbsp butter
1 lemon, juiced
2 tbsp white wine
2 tbsp chopped fresh rosemary or 1 tbsp dried
2 tbsp Italian parsley
4 garlic cloves, minced
1 tsp dry mustard
1 tsp paprika

1/8 tsp red pepper flakes
1 tsp salt
1/8 tsp ground black pepper

Preheat oven to 325 degrees.
Heat oil and butter in saucepan.
Add remaining ingredients and simmer for 5 minutes.
Baste chicken with the mixture.
Bake for 1 1/2 to 2 hours, or until juices run clear.
Allow it to sit for 15 minutes before carving.

There are cycles and trends in cooking just as there are in fashion. What is popular today can be dismissed tomorrow as tired and old. Then suddenly some chef somewhere rediscovers a recipe we've been making for years and declares it the next best thing. This proves we should all make what we like and not let anyone rob us of the dishes we enjoy most. Artichoke dip became popular about fifteen years ago. Then it fell out of favor and was deemed passé—along with avocado toast. It was a simple recipe my husband learned to make as an appetizer. It is still a favorite of ours; we serve it to guests along with French bread or crackers. There is never a morsel left over.

Hot Artichoke Dip

1 8.5-oz. can artichokes, packed in water, drained
1 can green chili
1 cup grated Parmesan cheese
1 cup mayonnaise

Preheat oven to 350 degrees.
Combine all ingredients.
Place in an ovenproof serving dish.
Bake for 30 minutes.
Let rest for 10 minutes before serving.
Makes 3 cups.

This is an easy, versatile topping for any fruit crisp baked in the oven. I first tasted it when we were visiting a farm family of fourteen during my first year of marriage. I was amazed at the amount of food that needed to be prepared for each meal. I watched with wonder as the daughters filled an enormous bowl with the ingredients and spread it on three pans of apples. For my use I cut the recipe way down. It still makes its way to our company table on top of apples, peaches, blueberries, or even rhubarb.

Goodie Topping

1 cup butter, melted
2 cups brown sugar
2 cups flour
3 cups oatmeal *(quick cooking, but any kind will do)*
1 tsp salt
1 tsp cinnamon
5 cups apples, peeled and sliced *(or other fruit. If using rhubarb, add more sugar, it must be added to the fruit along, with 2–3 tbsp flour.)*

Preheat oven to 350 degrees.

Place prepared fruit in a bowl and add 1/2 cup sugar and 1/2 tsp cinnamon, and 2 tbsp flour. When using apples I don't always add flour at this step. We don't mind a juicy bottom layer.

Layer fruit on the bottom of a greased 9x13-pan.

Spread the flour/oatmeal mixture over the top.

Bake for between 45–60 minutes, or until the top is golden and the fruit is bubbling and soft.

Don't let this desert's simplicity fool you. Its lemony flavor and texture make a special addition to any meal. If you use a store-bought frozen pie crust, it can be whipped up in just a few minutes.

Lemon Chess Pie

9-inch unbaked pie shell
4 eggs
1/4 cup milk
2 cups sugar
1 tbsp flour
1 tbsp cornmeal
1 tsp lemon zest
1/3 cup fresh lemon juice
1 stick melted butter

Heat oven to 425 degrees.

Add milk and eggs to a mixing bowl. Whisk or use an electric mixer to combine.

Mix together sugar, flour, and cornmeal. Gradually add flour mixture to the egg mixture while beating.

Add lemon juice, zest, and butter. Beat well.

Pour over the unbaked pie shell.

Place in oven and reduce heat to 300 degrees.

Bake until set—around 45–55 minutes.

Optional: Serve with whipped cream.

Here, during the Advent season, we hit the eggnog and the pecan fudge pretty hard, but if you want something good and aren't on some cruel version of the Atkin's Diet, something healthy and tasty, especially if made with organic ingredients, then make this. Or get someone to make it for you. You can eat this anytime in moderation. It makes a great Christmas gift for someone who has everything. Or nothing. It's from my friend, Mary Jane Clark, who'd be glad to share it. Mary Jane isn't around anymore. She's either resting, all healed from her cancer, or possibly she's eating her granola and laughing with her first husband, who left her via the windshield of a car one dark night when their children were small. In any case, I know nothing is dark for her now.

We used to eat this together in the morning, watching Mary Jane's cats stalk butterflies in her garden in the foothills of Colorado's San Juan Mountains. I think if you make this and eat it, you'll feel better about most things. You'll definitely be more regular and there is both irony and joy in that.

Mary Jane's Granola

12 cups regular *(thick-cut or traditional)* oatmeal
1 cup of each of the following:
Sesame seeds
Oat bran
Powdered milk *(optional)*
Sunflower seeds
Nuts *(pecans, cashews, whatever is on hand)*
2 cups coconut
1 tsp salt
2 tsp cinnamon *(optional)*

Preheat oven to 350 degrees. In a large bowl, combine the ingredients listed above, then in a small saucepan, heat the following until the sugar is dissolved.

1 tbsp vanilla
2/3 cup honey
2/3 cup brown sugar
2/3 cup olive oil
2/3 cup water

Add to oatmeal mixture. Stir until well-coated. Place in 9x13 cake pans *(makes 4 pans)*. Bake about 35 minutes until light brown and crisp, stirring several times. The recipe can easily be reduced. Before packaging in ziplock bags, add raisins, dried cranberries, or chopped dried apricots.

Several years ago, as a lark, I entered my strawberry-rhubarb pie into the Scott County Fair food contest. I was shocked to learn I not only won the blue ribbon for the fruit pie section, I won the grand championship for the entire pie category. However, two problems stole my initial pride. There were only three other fruit pies in my section. Plus, I had to brace myself when picking up the ribbons under the hostile eyes of the old-timer ladies who wondered how I, a newcomer, had the audacity to beat them. So here is that "award-winning" recipe for my husband's all-time favorite pie.

Strawberry-Rhubarb Pie

Pastry for a 9-inch two-crust pie
1 2/3 cup sugar
1/3 cup flour
2 cups fresh rhubarb cut in 1/2 inch pieces
2 cups fresh strawberries, sliced
Pinch of salt
2 tbsp butter

Preheat oven to 425 degrees.

In a large bowl mix all ingredients together. You can always be a little more generous with the amounts of fruit. I usually end up with about 5 cups.

Pour into a pie plate, dot with butter, and place the second crust on top. Make little slits in the top with a fork or knife to let steam escape.

Optional: Brush the top with cream or egg and sprinkle with sugar.

Bake for 10 minutes, then turn the oven down to 350 degrees and bake for another 40–45 minutes, or until the crust is brown and the filling is bubbling through the vents. Placing the pie on an old cookie sheet will spare you cleanup grief if it boils over in the oven.

Serve with vanilla ice cream.

Although this recipe appears in *The Exact Place* I've added it here again, in honor of my Grandma Frolander who made this pie for every holiday. I still miss her and wish I had said "I love you" more often than I did. This desert makes a perfect end to a feast because it is so light and airy. You always have room for a sweet serving of Angel Pie.

Grandma Frolander's Angel Pie

4 egg whites
1/4 tsp cream of tartar
1 cup sugar
4 egg yolks
1/2 cup sugar
1 lemon, juice and zest
1 cup cream, whipped, no sugar added.

Beat egg whites and until foamy. Gradually add cream of tartar and sugar, beating until meringue stands in stiff peaks. Spread in a buttered 9-inch pie plate. Bake at 275 for one or two hours or longer until crust is dry all the way through. Turn oven off and allow crust to cool in the oven.

In a saucepan beat yolks until thick. Add sugar and lemon. Stirring constantly, thicken over medium heat.

Spread 1/2 the whipped cream on top of cooled meringue. Carefully spread lemon filling as the next layer. Spread remaining whipped cream on top of filling. Refrigerate until served.

ENDNOTES

CONSIDER THIS

1 Anonymous, "Lo, How a Rose E'er Blooming," trans. Theodore Baker, accessed July 10, 2021, https://hymnary.org/text/lo_how_a_rose_eer_blooming.

PARENTING. I'M DONE

1 Doriani, Dan and Jack Collins. "Rearing Covenant Children in Faith." *Sincerely Yours: A Publication of Covenant Theological Seminary* 3, no. 2 (1996).

DEATH COMES FOR A BISHOP

1 *Book of Common Prayer* (Oxford Press, 2007), 41.
2 Hilaire Belloc, *Cranmer, Archbishop of Canterbury, 1533–1556* (UK: J.B. Lippincott, 1931).
3 Belloc, *Cranmer.*
4 *Book of Common Prayer,* 334.
5 A base, cowardly, or despicable person.
6 The Ex-Classics Website, 331 Thomas Cranmer from *Fox's Book of Martyrs*
7 Todd, Henry John. *The Life of Archbishop Cranmer,* Vol II. London: Gilber and Rivington, 1831. 499-504.
8 Adapted from *Sketches From Church History,* by S.M. Houghton (UK: Banner of Truth, 1980) and *Thomas Cranmer, Theologian,* by G.W. Bromiley (UK: Oxford University Press, 1956).

COOL COTTON SHEETS

1 *Letters of Samuel Rutherford* by Samuel Rutherford (Banner of Truth Trust; 1973)

DO NOT OPEN UNDER PRESSURE

1 J.R.R. Tolkien, *The Hobbit* (New York: Mariner Books, 1937, repub. 2012), 48–49.
2 J.R.R. Tolkien, *The Fellowship of the Ring* (New York: HarperCollins, 1954, repub. 2014), 203.
3 Saint Francis de Sales Quotes https://quotefancy.com/saint-francis-de-sales-quotes

CALL THE FBI

1 David Hilfiker, "When Mental Illness Blocks the Spirit," on David Hilfiker's official website, accessed July 5, 2021, http://www.davidhilfiker.com/index.php?option=com_content&view=article&id=33:when-mental-illness-blocks-the-spirit&catid=14:spirituality-essays&Itemid=24.
2 For further reading, note an interview with Oliver Sacks (also author of *Awakenings* which was made into a movie starring Robin Williams): "The Fully Immersive Mind of Oliver Sacks," by Steve Silberman, *WIRED Magazine,* August 31, 2015, https://www.wired.com/2015/08/fully-immersive-mind-oliver-sacks/.

EATING THE EASTER BUNNY

1 Thomas Keller was chef and owner of the French Laundry, a famous restaurant in the Napa Valley of California.
2 Michael Rhulman, "Natural-Born Keller" *in Best Food Writing 2000* (New York: Marlowe, 2000).
3 *Critique* was a publication written and edited by my husband, Denis. *Notes From Toad Hall* was a personal essay and ministry update written by me. Dividing our mailing list so a person would receive only one or the other was too complicated and costly for our small organization.

ENDNOTES

I WANT WHAT THE CAT ATE

1 Eugene Peterson, "Transparent Lives: The Slow but Urgent Work of Contemplation," *Christian Century,* November 29, 2003, https://www.christiancentury.org/article/2003-11/transparent-lives.

DOWN THE RABBIT HOLE

1 *Popular Science,* "Cult Science: Dressing up Mysticism as Quantum Physics." by Gregory Mone, Oct 20,2004

CALM DOWN

1 Sufjan Stevens, "Come Thou Fount," from *Songs for Christmas* (Asthmatic Kitty Records, 2005).

2 Julie Powell, *Julie & Julia* (New York: Little, Brown, 2005), 305.

REFLECTIONS ON WORK

1 "Vocation Prayer," in *Saint Meinrad Prayer Book* (Saint Meinrad Alumni Association, 1995).

2 Gerard Manley Hopkins, "The Principle or Foundation," in *Gerard Manley Hopkins: The Major Works,* ed. Catherine Phillips (New York: Oxford University Press, reissued 2009), 292.

3 From the film documentary *Leonard Cohen: I'm Your Man,* directed by Lian Lunson (Sundance Channel, 2005).

4 John Calvin on Luke 10:38, in *Calvin's Commentary on Matthew, Mark, Luke, Vol 2* (Grand Rapids, MI: Christian Classics Ethereal Library).

5 Frederick Buechner, *Wishful Thinking: A Theological ABC* (New York: Harper & Row, 1973).

6 Noelle Oxenhandler, "Fall From Grace: How Modern Life Has Made Waiting a Desperate Act," *New Yorker,* June 16, 1997, https://www.newyorker.com/magazine/1997/06/16/fall-from-grace.

7 Terry Cummins, *Feed My Sheep* (self-published, 2003), 47.

8 Gail Sher, *One Continuous Mistake: Four Noble Truths for Writers* (New York: Penguin, 1999), 58–59.

A DIARY OF LITTLE MATTERS

1 Jane Austen, Emma (UK: 1815).

2 A software program for banking and bill paying.

3 James Houston, *Joyful Exiles: Life in Christ on the Dangerous Edge of Things* (Downers Grove, IL: InterVarsity Press, 2007), 129.

4 It is a scientific fact. The sweat and oil of *some* bodies (not only male bodies) cause sheets and pillows to stain yellow.

SKIRTING THE FLEECE

1 Sue Johnson, *Hold Me Tight* (London: Piatkus Books, 2011), 47.

A NUTMEG OF CONSOLATION

1 Georgius Everhardus Rumphius, *The Ambonese Herbal,* trans. E.M. Beekman (New Haven, CT: Yale University Press, 2011).

2 Initially published by Kalos Press, *The Exact Place* was revised and republished by Square Halo Books in 2021.

3 *Letters of John Calvin,* (First published in 1855-7) Selected from the Bonnet Edition, (The Banner of Truth Trust, 1980) page 154-155.

4 *The Complete Aubrey/Maturin Novels,* Vol. iv by Patrick O'Brian "The Nutmeg of Consolation" 1991, (Norton & Company 2004) page 454.

ENDNOTES

TOOTHPASTE IN THE TOILET

1 Bruce Ray Smith, *Winter Light: A Christian's Search for Humility* (Kalos Press, 2011), 17.

2 Smith, *Winter Light,* 22.

SAY "I LOVE YOU"

1 Ellis Potter, *Three Theories of Everything* (Destinée Media, 2012), 106.

THE MOUNTAIN ASH

1 Linford Detweiler and Karin Bergquist, "'We Grow Songs': Over the Rhine on Making Untamed Music," interview by David Greene, NPR, August 30, 2013, https://www.npr.org/2013/08/30/214828307/we-grow-songs-over-the-rhine-on-making-untamed-music.

2 This did end up getting written, and was published in 2021 as *No Place: A Desert Pilgrimage.*

EVERY LITTLE THING

1 Parker Palmer, *Let Your Life Speak: Listening for the Voice of Vocation* (San Francisco, CA: Jossey-Bass, 2000).

A GENTLE MADNESS

1 "The Things They Brought Back," *National Geographic,* January 2014, https://www.nationalgeographic.com/magazine/article/things-brought-back.

2 Mary Pipher, *Another Country: Navigating the Emotional Terrain of Our Elders* (New York: Riverhead Books, 1999).

3 J.I. Packer, *Knowing God* (Downers Grove, IL: InterVarsity Press, 1973), 37.

4 Shane Claiborne, Jonathan Wilson-Hartgrove, and Enuma Okoro, *Common Prayer: A Liturgy for Ordinary Radicals* (Grand Rapids, MI: Zondervan, 2010), 115.

5 Claiborne, Wilson-Hartgrove, and Okoro, *Common Prayer,* 120.

SPRING, PLEASE COME

1 Mary Pipher, *Another Country: Navigating the Emotional Terrain of Our Elders* (New York: Riverhead Books, 1999).

2 Pipher, *Another Country,* 32.

3 Our ministry, Ransom Fellowship, has a Board of Directors who keep us legal and to whom we are accountable. They help set policy and budget, but they are also dear friends who have walked with us for many years.

4 Sarah Susanka, *The Not So Big House: A Blueprint for the Way We Really Live* (Newtown, CT: Taunton Press, 2001).

EPILOGUE

1 Daniel Taylor, *Creating a Spiritual Legacy: How to Share Your Stories, Values, and Wisdom* (Grand Rapids, MI: Brazos Press, 2011).

2 Frederick Buechner, *Telling Secrets: A Memoir* (New York: HarperCollins, 1991).

3 J.I. Packer, *Knowing God* (Downers Grove, IL: InterVarsity Press, 1973), 37.

About the Author

MARGIE HAACK is a writer living in Savage, MN, with her husband Denis, on a half-acre lot next to a wooded park where she tries to attract bumble bees and hummingbirds with marginal success. Nature and place connect her to the spiritual geography that has shaped her. She has a deep love for home and hospitality, art and culture, and an awareness of God's presence in everyday life. It has been her persistent quest to name what is holy, what is funny, and what is suffering in the ordinary and routine. She and her husband delight in three adult children, their spouses, nine grandchildren, and a great-grandson. Between 1983 and 2020 they worked as directors of Ransom Fellowship, a ministry encouraging Christians to learn to be discerning, and to live faithfully in the midst of our culture. Besides the *Place* trilogy, Margie's writing has appeared in *Arthouse America, Comment Magazine* and other publications. You can find both Margie and Denis' writing at *Critique-Letters.com.*

Acknowledgments

I am thankful for many great writers whose work represented voices as different from one another as Minnesota is from Hawaii. From Anne Lamott's hilarious memoirs to Cormac McCarthy's minimalist, sometimes violent fiction, I have learned from and been inspired by them. They gave me courage to embrace my own voice.

From my heart I salute the readers who loyally followed *Notes From Toad Hall* over the years and who often responded with stories of their own. Without their encouragement, I would have quit long ago. Thank you for sticking with me.

While Denis and I directed Ransom Fellowship, our Board was always supportive and glad to have *Notes From Toad Hall,* which later became *Letters from the House Between,* represent a voice from our ministry. They never flagged in their enthusiasm.

I am delighted Ned Bustard became my editor and publisher. He believed in this project even before it was published the first time as *God in the Sink.* He was not willing to let it go when it went out of print. He foresaw this book as part of a trilogy that would become *This Place* and insisted we add new chapters.

Thea Rosenburg's proofreading and editorial skills are exceptional. She patiently smoothed rough edges and strengthened the stories I set out to tell. She deserves a gold medal for all the punctuation changes that needed to be made.

Isabel and Daniel Bixby rescued this manuscript from its old life as *God in the Sink* by reformatting and reentering it. They saved me hours and hours of work that would have driven me crazy.

I am deeply grateful for Andi, Katy, and Peggy who kept praying, when I was in the process of putting this collection together. When I saw the accumulated me, I was so disheartened I wanted to jump off the project. With patience and kindness they prayed me to safer ground.

Anita Gorder's gracious help made it easier to focus knowing supper was on its way on days when I was on a roll and needed to continue writing. Thank you.

Special thanks to our children, their spouses, and our grandchildren. Without the richness of the experiences they give, I would be barren and poor. I can't imagine life without them.

Marsena Adams-Dufresne's editing skills made this made this manuscript so much better than it was. She had an eye for both the big picture and the details and that kept me confident as I pulled all this together. As a result it became more fluid and compelling. I love how she loves the Chicago Manuel of Style and yet was able to shine it on when it didn't fit my style.

Finally, Denis. He has been my most faithful supporter and believer in the writing gift God has given me. In the early years when he critiqued my writing, that I insisted I wanted, he persevered in spite of my hostility. There were many times I wanted to give up writing because each issue of *Notes* precipitated a crisis between us, not because of what I wrote about us—he was always a pretty good sport about that—but because I couldn't take criticism. It took years to accept it gracefully and to agree with him when he said: "You really are a writer." Thank you, love.

A good PLACE to find some great books . . . .

THE EXACT PLACE: A SEARCH FOR FATHER
—BOOK ONE OF THE *PLACE* TRILOGY

"Margie tells the story of her childhood and of the discovery of the kindness of God and the meaning of home. As I read the story of young Margie's life, I reflected on my own, and wondered at the goodness in the ordinary—land well-tended, food well-prepared, children sheltered and fed with sweat and tears—and at the unfolding of hope in the midst of hardship and heartbreak."

—**Gideon Strauss, academic dean of the Institute for Christian Studies**

NO PLACE: A DESERT PILGRIMAGE
—BOOK TWO OF THE *PLACE* TRILOGY

"In *No Place,* Margie tells her story of becoming. Weaving through joy and through pain, through periods of confidence and bewilderment, the story's persistent thread is Margie seeking Jesus while befriending others wit compassion. Written with humility, humor, and the unique insight gained from a rare path taken, Margie invites us to join her as she finds her place of service "among the hippies and the stoners, the Jesus freaks and the drop-outs," learns her rhythm of hospitality as an act of Christian faith, and grows into a profound wisdom.

—**Nancy Nordenson, author *Finding Livelihood: A Progress of Work and Leisure***

GODLY CHARACTER(S): INSIGHTS FOR SPIRITUAL PASSION
FROM THE LIVES OF 8 WOMEN IN THE BIBLE

". . . these 'great eight' propel you towards habits of godliness—putting you in a place to receive grace and fall more deeply in love with your savior—and that in His love you might be re-shaped and re-formed."

—**Robert William Alexander, author of *The Gospel-Centered Life at Work***

A BOOK FOR HEARTS & MINDS: WHAT YOU SHOULD READ AND WHY

"Curators of the imagination, stewards of the tradition, priests of print, [Hearts & Minds Bookstore has] always done more than sold books: they have furnished faithful minds and hearts. This book is a lovely testimony to that good work."

—**James K.A. Smith, Calvin College, author of *You Are What You Love: The Spiritual Power of Habit***

NAMING THE ANIMALS: AN INVITATION TO CREATIVITY

"A lovely primer about our collective call to be creative. Accessible to all, Roach and Bustard's book sets readers on a path toward deeper exploration into the role of creativity within our Christian walk."

—**Lawan Glasscock, Christians in the Visual Arts (CIVA)**

Square Halo Books.com